abortion?

Resources for Pastoral Counseling

abortion?

Resources for Pastoral Counseling

Eldon Weisheit

Publishing House
St. Louis

Concordia Publishing House, St. Louis, Missouri
Copyright © 1976 Concordia Publishing House
Manufactured in the United States of America

Library of Congress Cataloging in Publication Data

Weisheit, Eldon.
    Abortion? : Resources for pastoral counseling.

    Bibliography: p.
    1. Abortion. 2. Abortion—Religious   aspects. 3. Pastoral
counseling. I. Title.
HQ767.3.W45   259   75-43587
ISBN 0-570-03259-8

Contents

PREFACE

This book started as (and in a paperback version still is) an inexpensive book for those who are considering an abortion—one that dealt with the process of reaching a decision rather than proving which decision was right. The idea was to have a book that could be placed in libraries and made available in other places for those who are concerned about the subject. Though anyone facing the possibility of an abortion should have a professional person as a counselor, the fact is, many people can talk to no one about such an important decision. Maybe a book written directly to the pregnant woman would be of some help.

The marketing research people at Concordia Publishing House agreed. But during their research, they came up with another idea. Many counselors might use the book for their own sessions with a person who wished to discuss abortion. The counselor might use ideas from the book—selecting only those that applied to the specific situation—or might loan the book to the counselee. However, the research also showed that the counselors would want more information than was in the original manuscript.

So one book became two. The first book is included as Part One of this book. It is intended for the counselee. You decide on the best method to share it with the person who has come to you for help. Loan her this copy. Buy the paperback version where you got this one and give her a copy. Or just use the outline as a way to get conversations going.

Part Two of this book is for you as a counselor. It will remind you of some things you already knew. It will give you food for thought as you work with the problem of a decision regarding abortion. But unlike the arithmetic books we had in school way back then, the answer is not in the back of the book. No simple solution has been found for the question of abortion.

Since you are reading this book, I have assumed you have not arrived at one solution on the abortion issue for all who come to you for counsel. I hope this book and the resources it suggests will help you in your struggle. If you have arrived at a final answer (and are only reading this to see if I agree with you), I hope this will help you understand those who have arrived at different answers. I want to share with you what has happened to me during the time I have worked on these two manuscripts.

I started the first book, *Should I Have an Abortion?*, shortly after I left a congregation and community where I frequently counseled with people about abortion. As I did my writing, several women who knew about my project came to me and shared their own decisions on the subject. During that time I accepted the possibility and probability of many abortions.

But during the year I have talked about and worked on the second manuscript, I have been a step farther away from frontline counseling. My ministry has taken me into other fields. Abortion became a subject for coffee-break discussions and material from books for a book. During this year I have become much more antiabortion.

I share this with you because I have discovered something about myself that deeply concerns me. It could also happen to you. I have found that as long as I deal with abortion (or it could be one of many other subjects) academically and theoretically, it is easier to give absolute answers. I have read enough that I can think I am right; then I know I am right—and that is not good.

On the other hand, I recognize that prior to doing this research I counseled on a serious subject about which, I now have found, I knew very little. During those years of parish ministry I was very much involved with the issue of abortion, but I was not as well prepared to give needed help as I should have been.

So I am a part of, and I assume you are too, the age-old struggle between the practical and the theoretical. If you are in that tension, I urge you not to lose your grip on either position. Hold on to both and you will help many people.

Eldon Weisheit

PART I

CHAPTER 1
Something to Think About

For the person considering an abortion, there are two easy answers:

ANSWER 1: I would never get an abortion under any circumstance. Abortion is murder.

ANSWER 2: I'd get an abortion any time I needed and wanted one. Abortion is no different than having a tooth pulled.

Those who have already accepted either position don't have to do any more thinking about the subject. They have already made their decision. However, such absolute statements are most often made by men, or by nonpregnant and nonimpregnable women. Most women who become pregnant when they don't want to give birth to a child are not so fast in giving an answer regarding abortion.

Look at All Answers

However, the choice is not just between Answer 1 and Answer 2. There are many other opinions about abortion that fall on a scale between the two absolutes. If you are to consider any of these other views, you must be willing to think about the subject of abortion. You must, first of all, consider both the possibilities—it is possible that you might have an abortion (others have), and it is possible that you might not have an abortion (others haven't). You will have to sort out your feelings, establish your priorities, and consider the long-range results of your decision.

Thinking about all the issues involved in deciding to have or not to have an abortion is not easy. It might seem easier, for the moment anyway, to shut your eyes and grab either Answer 1 or Answer 2. However when you consider more than just the present moment but also the future months and years, it is better to think through the impact this decision will have on your life. You might feel it's not worth the emotional expense of facing long lists of difficult questions when you know the final decision must be either abortion: yes or abortion: no. With the 50 percent chance of picking the right answer anyway, you might decide to depend on luck and save yourself all the anguish of logically and emotionally making a decision.

But the reason for working through a series of questions to reach a decision is not to find a formula that will give you a quick and obvious answer. You will probably find good reasons for taking either course. Nor do you go through a process of decision making in order to change your mind—though you have to be open to that possibility. The purpose of your thinking through a number of issues regarding yourself and your decision is to help you adjust your life to whatever decision you do reach. By thinking through the matter now, before you take action, you will be better equipped to accept and make the best of your present situation.

So an abortion is something to think about.

Find Someone to Talk To

Ideally, you should do this thinking with someone else. When you share your ideas with others, you have a better chance to evaluate them yourself. Sometimes what seems sensible when you think it, sounds foolish when you say it. Try to find someone you feel free to talk to—not someone who will tell you what to do but someone who will help you understand your own feelings.

Since I am a pastor, I naturally would recommend that you discuss this with a minister. But that depends on you and what your view of ministers is. It also depends on the kind of ministry available to you. Find a pastor you can talk to. Other people you might want to talk with are suggested in later

14

chapters. Remember, this book is not a substitute for human relationships. I hope I can talk to you via the printed page, but I also want you to have someone to talk to. In the long run I feel I would be more helpful if I could listen to you rather than speak to you. But no one has yet invented a book that will offer two-way communication.

Have Your Views Changed?

To get the conversation started, let's go back to the two extreme answers regarding abortion. Even though you do not accept either answer completely, you probably lean more toward one than the other.

If you feel totally confused about the subject now, think back to six months ago. What would you have said about abortion then? Being pregnant and unhappy about it may have changed your views. That's okay. We can all have strong views on subjects we are not personally involved in. But when the situation becomes real in our own lives, we often find our views changing. Sometimes what seemed like simple problems aren't so simple anymore. But try to remember what you thought about abortion before you faced the problem yourself. Your previous views and how they may have changed will help you understand how your attitudes vary with the situation. You can then be aware that your views may change again—so keep that possiblity in mind as you consider this issue.

To make it easier, let's change Answer 1 and Answer 2 slightly by making the first, "I really don't like the idea of abortion, but maybe there are times when it is necessary." And the second is, "I think in most cases a person should be free to get an abortion if she wants, but she should consider a lot of things first."

Opposed to Abortion?

First, let's assume you feel nearer Answer 1—you don't like the idea of an abortion. You should list your reasons why you are opposed to abortion. Remember, our concern goes beyond whether or not you get the abortion. The reasons you give to yourself and other for your decision will have a big influence on the rest of your life. So examine your reasons and see if they are valid and if they are important to you.

Medical Problems

Some are against abortion on medical grounds. Abortions in the past were often done under illegal and unsanitary conditions. For those reasons many women died from abortions and others developed medical problems that prevented them from having children later. If less than adequate medical services are available to you, then by all means avoid an abortion. The physical, psychological, and legal hazards of such an abortion are too great.

But most abortions no longer have to be done under improper medical conditions—unless there are special problems of secrecy involved.

However, there are also dangers in *not* getting an abortion only because you are afraid of the medical conditions involved in the procedure. If fear prevents you from getting an abortion, you may later have a strong resentment against the child born from your pregnancy. Remove doubts about the medical factors involved—not just so you will be free to have an abortion but also so you will be free from not having one for the wrong reasons.

Those who are against abortion have explained in detail, with words and pictures, the various methods of abortion. An actual abortion was shown on television—in color. The clinical details of the surgery make most nonmedical people ill. But the details of other medical practices—from tooth extraction to open-heart surgery—are not subjects for mealtime conversation either. The gory details are not valid reasons to be opposed to abortion.

Against the Law?

In the past people were unable to have legal abortions except for special medical reasons. Many abortion laws have been declared unconstitutional. But the final word has not been written regarding the legality of abortions. Groups both for and against more liberalized abortion laws are at work.

But the availability of legal abortions on demand does not mean every pregnant women will get an abortion any more than laws against abortion prevented all surgical terminations of pregnancy. You needed a better reason for having a child than the fact that an abortion was illegal. For example, I hope the reason you do not rob banks is not just that it's against the law. A better reason is that you don't want to rob the bank. Laws are necessary, but they do change. Your sense of values should be higher than national or state laws.

Discussions about the medical and legal aspects of abortion often become impersonal. They must be considered in the broad sense of influencing the views of society, but now we are not arguing the total case of abortion. Now we are concerned about one situation—your own. You are a part of society and influenced by others. But you must consider your individual role in society. If you are convinced abortion is wrong, do not go against your conscience and seek an abortion. But search for positive reasons for having a child rather than fear of the consequences of abortion or its nonavailability. If you don't want an abortion, then continue your pregnancy and give birth to a child, not because you are forced to, but because you want to.

Moral Grounds

Many are opposed to abortion on spiritual and moral grounds. Face the big question: Do I feel an abortion destroys a human life? A "yes" answer does not mean you will not get an abortion. All of us know that certain acts are wrong, yet that knowledge has not always prevented us from doing them. The Biblical writer St. Paul identifies with the problem when he says, "For I do not do the good I want, but the evil I do not want is what I do." (Romans 7:19)

A spiritual conviction against abortion and for life is a positive reason for not ending a pregnancy. Your relationship

17

with God regarding abortion will be discussed in a later chapter. At this point you are to think about your reasons for being opposed to abortion so you might build positive reasons for continuing a pregnancy.

Are You Tempted?

If you are opposed to abortion on moral grounds, you may regard any discussion on the subject as temptation. If abortion is wrong, then to consider it is to be tempted. So let's talk a little about temptation.

Often people feel guilty about being tempted. Temptation is a reminder of weakness. It opens the door to the possibility of serious sin. When we admit we are tempted, we are admitting our desire to do something wrong.

Feeling guilty about temptation cuts us off from the two best weapons against temptation—prayer and pastoral counseling. If you think it is already sin to be tempted, how can you talk to either God or people about it? It's almost like asking for permission to sin. Many people are afraid to pray about temptation because they don't want God brought in on the case when they know they may end up doing wrong. Many won't talk to a pastor because they think his only answer would be to say, "Don't do it."

But that attitude misunderstands both temptation and God's love. The answer to temptation is not to hide from it or to pretend it is not there. The answer is to expose it—to look not just for a yes or no answer but for the reason. Because of my own guilt feelings about being tempted I remember the joy of finding an idea in the New Testament letter to the Hebrews. I'd like to share it with you: "For we have not a high priest [that is, Christ] who is unable to sympathize with our weaknesses, but one who in every respect has been tempted as we are, yet without sinning." (Hebrews 4:15)

First of all, temptation in itself is not sin. Christ was tempted in all ways that we are tempted. Yet He did not sin. You are not guilty because you are tempted to do something wrong.

18

Next, Christ understands us because He has been tempted as we are tempted. He became a human like us to share even the problems of our lives. Don't let Christ's maleness prevent you from receiving comfort regarding abortion from this promise. Christ could not have been tempted to have an abortion in the way you might be tempted. But He loved then, as He does now, women who suffered such temptation. A husband who loves his pregnant wife may regard the possibility of an abortion as a temptation. The father or brother of an unmarried pregnant woman can regard abortion as a temptation. As I share your concerns about an unwanted pregnancy, I am tempted to see abortion as the fastest, easiest way out of the problem. No man can claim that he feels the problem of abortion as a woman does. But don't feel "nobody understands me" and use that as a self-made barrier to keep others from helping. Christ, above all, has broken that barrier down. He knows about temptation. That's why He is here. You can let Him in on the problem.

The best way to defeat temptation is to face it. The spiritual values involved will be discussed later. For now, think about the problem without feeling guilty about being tempted. Guilt will only make your decision more difficult and add to your own problems. By honestly facing the issue of abortion as a temptation, you can use the resources that are available to resist it. You can know that God loves and understands you. You can talk to Him and listen to Him. You can share your feelings with others and listen to their views.

What's Wrong with Abortion?

But what if your view is nearer Answer 2? You feel basically that abortion is permissible, but you are not sure about your own situation. If you do not feel that abortion is, in itself, morally wrong, you may have been turned off by the talk about temptation. I ask you to reconsider. There is no easy answer to the abortion question. The fact that legal, medical, and theological authorities disagree and the fact that publishers still think books like this are necessary show that

19

the problem has not been solved. (Same little pep talk goes for those who feel in their hearts that abortion is wrong. You may not like the approach of those with other views. But looking at another side of the issue may help you understand your own position better.)

An illustration: Some people feel it is wrong to drink any alcohol. Others think there is no sin in drinking alcohol, but that intoxication is wrong. Then there are the degrees between, ranging from those who accept a glass of wine on special occasions to those who think a person isn't drunk until he is flat on the floor. Though each person may be convinced he or she is right regarding the use of alcohol, each must learn to live with people with different opinions. There is a similar range of views on abortion. Some feel there is nothing wrong in having an abortion during the first three months of pregnancy. Other have a different time schedule, but agree there is a point in the pregnancy when an abortion would be wrong. There is always a moral decision involved in abortion—even for those who believe in abortion on demand.

Are You in Favor of THIS Abortion?

Though you may believe that abortion is a medical rather than a moral question, there is still the problem of whether or not *you* should have an abortion.

The movie (or novel, if you read rather than watch) *Airport* includes a subplot about the relationship of a stewardess and a pilot married to another woman. Early in the film she tells him she is pregnant by him, and he assumes she will have an abortion. She says she had always thought she would seek an abortion if their relationship resulted in her becoming pregnant. But when she discovered her situation, she had doubts. She thought she wanted to have the child.

There could be many variations of the same plot—and you might be one of them. If you have previously expressed your approval of abortion (when you were not personally involved), go back and look at the reasons you gave favoring

20

abortion. Do this to determine whether your reasons now apply to your situation. No one (at least I assume no one) is in favor of aborting every pregnancy. Those who are fighting for abortion on demand want the right for each woman to make her own decision. Even though you led a demonstration opposing antiabortion laws, even if you are the president of the Planned Parenthood League, you do not have to get an abortion just because you are pregnant. In a small sense you are facing the freedom that many have struggled for all women to have. But now you must make the decision on the issues involving you. To prove that you have the right to do it is not a proper reason to terminate a pregnancy.

Those who favor abortion on demand often state that abortion laws are unfair because they discriminate against the poor. Women who can pay the price can get around the law. Those who can't, either have no abortion or fall into the hands of illegal and unsanitary abortion mills. The argument is true. As a nation (and as states) we need to reevaluate our legal system regarding abortions. Laws that were made to protect life have, at times, destroyed life.

But the struggle to have more justice in abortion laws is not against a moral code. It is for a moral code fair to all. People who have this freedom must use it with responsibility. They must act in a way that does not fill them with regrets later. They must think about their own decisions rather than have a law make their decisions for them.

Personal or Collective Decision?

Some argue against strict abortion laws because they feel it is a personal, individual decision rather than a legal decision of the community or government. We will discuss the it's-my-body-I'll-do-what-I-want-with-it argument in detail later. Now let's face the basic conflict regarding individual versus government decisions.

On the one hand we make laws that forbid certain acts: murder, stealing, kidnapping, racial discrimination, even speeding. Many did argue that racial discrimination was a personal matter, not a legal one. "You can't legislate morality," was used as an argument against civil rights laws. Yet in the other areas all (well, almost all) agree that we need rules to establish moral conduct. The Bible tells about a time when the people of Israel (they could hardly be called a nation at the time) went through political, social, and spiritual disintegration. It says of that period of history that each person did what was right in his own eyes. And chaos reigned. They had to establish laws by which they could create an order for them to live by. We have agreed and have established laws that determine moral conduct in our nation and our communities.

On the other hand, laws are not established for each moral issue. Old laws requiring church attendance, forbidding work on Sunday, punishing those who swear in the presence of ladies, forbidding the sale of alcohol, all have been dropped. Such subjects may still be moral issues for some, but the individual must decide his own moral action.

Where is the dividing line between what should be public morality and what should be private morality? That problem is far beyond the scope of this book. But the struggle about abortion as a legal question is a part of that effort to maintain a balance between personal freedom and public accountability.

Though you may have the legal right to have an abortion, you may have a moral responsibility not to. Just as there must be a better reason for not getting an abortion than because it is against the law, there also must be a better reason for getting an abortion than because it is legal.

Look for More Than One Answer

Specific reasons for which you may want an abortion will be considered in the next chapter. For now think about the reasons why you favor abortion in general, and see if the reasons apply to your situation. Then you are back to the idea of this chapter again: Do your own thinking, but consider all the issues. Views that you established on a political or social basis might not apply to an individual pregnancy. That does not mean you were wrong on the wider issue. It only means you are an individual.

What's in Between?

Perhaps your views on abortion were half way between Answer 1 and Answer 2. Maybe you never thought much about abortion because you never dreamed you would face such a decision. You might have felt it was better to stay neutral on the subject rather than offend someone who had strong opinions on either side.

But you can no longer stay neutral. You must give up your place in the "undecided" column of the public opinion poll. Now is the time for you to establish the home rules by which you will come to a decision. Your final action or nonaction will be determined by the questions you ask yourself and the priorities you establish. Perhaps no one can consider all the possible facts and feelings that should be considered regarding abortion. I am aware that this book won't cover all the bases. But each woman (I hope with the help of others) facing an abortion or a birth that she might not want must consider all the issues that affect her now and will affect her in the future.

Examine the concerns regarding abortion presented in the rest of this book. They are here to guide you in your thinking. But don't be limited by this book. Read other things that may come closer to your needs and your experience. Find people who understand you. Find others who have the medical, legal, or spiritual abilities you need. And pray.

CHAPTER 2
Who Wants to Be Pregnant?

Your first step in thinking about an abortion is to recognize where you are—pregnant and not happy about it.

What's the Question?

Why don't you want to be pregnant? Or maybe the question is: Why don't you want a baby? Or is the question: Why don't you want a baby at this time?

Deciding which question you will answer is already a step toward understanding your situation. Before you answer the question of your choice, give it some serious reflection.

Several months ago, before you were pregnant, the question would have been different. Then someone might have asked you if you wanted a baby and you could easily have said no. If you felt a need to explain why you didn't want to have a child at that time, you might have given some of the reasons that you would now give as reasons for wanting an abortion. The same needs, fears, problems that make you want to prevent a birth could also have made you want to prevent a pregnancy. But before you were pregnant your answer could have been given without as much introspection. You might have said, "I'm just not sure I want a baby." Or you might not have given any thought to the subject; but since you felt no strong urge to have a child, you simply had not planned to become pregnant. When you weren't pregnant, you didn't have to think of or give anyone else a reason for remaining that way.

The Answer Is for You

But now you're in a different situation. Remaining

24

nonpregnant is different than becoming unpregnant. Doctors and other counselors will ask why you want to terminate your pregnancy. Often such questions are required before an abortion can be performed. Even if you were not asked an official reason for wanting an abortion, you must have an answer for yourself. And the answer must be one you can live with. It must be acceptable to you not only now but also later. You may feel compelled to tell others your reasons for an abortion, and it will be important to be able to give reasons you believe. It is also true that you will have to have a reason for not having an abortion—a reason that you can accept yourself. Therefore, don't be hostile or evasive about the question, "Why will I do what I do?" An acceptable and honest answer now will help you later.

Often we make up our minds about something and then look for reasons to support our decision. That can be true for simple things, such as buying clothes, and for important decisions, such as choice of job or spouse. The "decide now, think later" policy shows that emotions have an important role in our decision making. And we can be grateful for the influence of emotions on our lives. People are made to be both emotional and logical. It's when a person becomes only one or the other that the balance is lost. The decision on abortion cannot be totally a logical process by which you make a list of reasons why you should, another list of why you shouldn't, and the longer list wins. Nor is it a totally emotional experience that says, "I feel like having an abortion," or "I'm scared to have an abortion." As we look at logical reasons for and against abortion, do not eliminate your emotional feelings. Be emotional about your logic and logical about your emotions. That's not an exact formula, but it's something you can use as a guideline.

Unwanted Pregnancy or Unwanted Child?

The first question is the easiest: Why don't you want to be pregnant? Even from a man's point of view I can think of reasons why a woman would dislike being pregnant. Despite all the public relations for pregnancy that assures women more beautiful skin and an inner glow while in that condition, and despite the new and improved maternity dresses, pregnancy has its drawbacks. If it's your first time through, you might have a lot of unnecessary fears about the nine-month waiting period. If you've been through it before, you might think, "Not again. I can't take the_____ (diet, morning sickness, exhaustion, walking like a duck, or whatever it was that crowded you against the wall the last time).

"Unwanted pregnancy" is a phrase well understood by women (and we men know the feeling too, if for different reasons). Though there are a few who skip through the nine months with the joys of a nest-builder, most pregnant women regard it as a burden.

But do you use the term "unwanted pregnancy" as a polite way of saying "unwanted child"? The two are not the same. Not wanting to be pregnant is one thing. Pregnancy is a terminal condition, less than ten months long. But an unwanted child is something else. A child will be with you for an average of 18 years—that may be about 30% of the memorable part of your life.

It's almost an oversimplification to suddently agree that it's the pregnancy and not a child that bothers you. But at least consider the possibility that your anxiety is caused by negative feelings about the discomfort of pregnancy rather than a baby. Many who don't want to be pregnant, want a baby very much.

Fears of Pregnancy

Even in this well-educated and, at least outwardly, enlightened generation many superstitions and old wives' tales still influence people's thinking. There was a time when a pregnant woman was not to be seen—it was her period of confinement. Because of a misunderstanding of Genesis 3 she may have thought it was her lot in life to suffer pain at childbirth. Your grandmother, or her mother, may well have been "churched" after each childbirth—that is, a special prayer was said so she would be "cleansed" for public worship again.

I hesitate to mention some of these negative views about pregnancy and childbirth because I am glad we have outgrown them. Women now lead active, productive (in other ways) lives while they are pregnant. My wife taught school through seven months of *our* first pregnancy. The teacher in the next room was even more pregnant—in quantity not quality. She had twins. It was a good experience for the children to be around active, pregnant women. Yet even today children may be influenced by stories told by grand-mothers, maiden aunts, and literature in a way that gives them a negative view of pregnancy and childbirth.

Remember back to the experiences that have given you your opinions on pregnancy. You might even make a list of the joys or tribulations of expecting a child. You may recognize that some of the joys of pregnancy are overstated, but more important you may see that some of your fears are not true. You may discover other worries about pregnancy that are valid. But there may also be something you can do about them. If you think you would have difficulties in childbirth because of a physical condition, ask a doctor. If you are worried that some illness or birth defect might be inherited from you, tell your doctor about your concerns. Separate your unnecessary anxieties from real problems. Then see what can be done about the real concerns.

Or "Not Now"?

But for most people "unwanted pregnancy" means "no children" at least for now. Let's look at some of the more common reasons why women, even those opposed to the idea of abortions, sometimes consider terminating a pregnancy. Some reasons may not apply to you. Skip them. Your individual situation may not be listed here—especially with the exact details that concern you. Use this list only as a base to start your thinking; then fill in all your special concerns to get a clear picture of your own need.

This list is not given to help you find an excuse for having an abortion. Nor are the ideas offered and then taken away to remove your reasons for ending your pregnancy. By sharing such a list two things should be obvious. First, other women have had the same problem and have regarded abortion as its solution. Second, others have faced the same problem and decided not to get an abortion. In no case is abortion the only choice you have. Abortion may be the first that comes to mind because it is the fastest way to be free from the worries you now have. But don't solve one problem by starting another.

Unwed Mother

First, and this used to be considered the only reason for abortions, let's consider the possibility that you are not married. Though in today's world married women also have abortions and unmarried women feel more free to have children; premarital pregnancy is still a major cause for women to request abortions.

There are obvious reasons why single women would not want a child. But not all the reasons apply to all unmarried women. Some are embarrassed and feel they have brought a great shame on themselves and the family. Often a single pregnant woman is afraid that her parents will disown her, that lives of younger brothers and sisters will be ruined, and that other relatives will never speak to her again. But don't assume you know how your family will react. And do not take action you think will solve their problem when they don't even know about the situation. Often parents react different-ly than you might expect. Your own attitude may be different than you thought it would be. Give them the chance to change from previously held views too.

Other unmarried pregnant women feel guilty about their condition. They feel they have sinned and the sin has been exposed to the whole world—or at least will be soon. There is a double standard regarding premarital sexual relationship and premarital pregnancies. Many will excuse, ignore, or defend sexual relationships outside of marriage, but will condemn pregnancy in the same case.

If you feel resentment toward that double standard as you face the choice of an abortion or a child with no father, don't let your anger add to your problem. Society (including you) has many double standards. They are unfair. But now is not the time for you to battle society's unfairness. You can name 17 girls who have been "sleeping around" for years and are not pregnant, and you can tell everyone that you did it only once. But that doesn't change the fact that you're the one pregnant. Do not solve guilt problems by pointing to others who are equally guilty.

Your relationship with the man who impregnated you will be discussed in more detail in the next chapter; for now, examine any feelings of guilt or shame you might have about your pregnancy. Is the guilt because of the sex act? The relationship? The pregnancy? Much that is expressed as guilt is often anger for being caught. But neither anger nor guilt is a good basis for a decision to abort. Nor is the feeling of "paying for my sin" by keeping the child a good basis for not having an abortion. You need to make your decision on solid, permanent feelings that will remain valid for you. To solve one temporary problem in a way that creates future problems is no help.

Good That Comes from Evil

The Old Testament story of Joseph and his brothers has helped me and might apply to you. The brothers sold Joseph as a slave. But from his position as slave Joseph rose to a high political office. The brothers came under the influence of his power and were afraid that he would seek revenge. But Joseph said, "You meant evil against me, but God meant it for good." What the brothers did was sinful. But the greatness of God's love is seen in the fact that He can make good come from a bad situation.

There may be sin involved in your pregnancy. But that's

29

not the issue now. God can make good come even from something that was evil. Many people (including me) can look back in their lives and see mistakes that could have destroyed all chances for happiness. But instead, good came from the wrong. That does not mean it is right to do wrong. It means that God has a lot of patience and is always willing to help us start over.

If you feel guilt or anger about your pregnancy, work out that problem now. Then from the base of forgiveness and hope you can make better decisions regarding your future.

There are other reasons why an unmarried woman might want an abortion. Perhaps she cannot support a child herself—especially if she loses work (maybe even her job) during the pregnancy. Unfair though it may be, a man does not have to face this part of the problem. Some men (may their numbers increase) have a sense of responsibility regarding their role as an unwed parent. But they do not face the physical impossibility of working during and after childbirth.

You will have to take an honest account of what your situation is. Who can help you? Who will? Many people who are willing to give advice about abortions are unwilling to give financial help if you decide against ending the pregnancy. Don't let their insincerity frustrate you. You may be disappointed that some from whom you expected help refused to stick with you. But there may be others who, to your surprise, come through in the time of need. There are also church agencies, public agencies, and funds to help unwed mothers. Abortion is not the only possible solution. Consider others.

An unmarried woman may also want to avoid forcing a man to marry her because she is pregnant. And she is right— pregnancy is not a good reason for getting married. If a couple plans to get married and they find she is pregnant, then the possibility of a child is not the cause for the marriage and it should not be a cause to prevent a marriage. But marriages established "to give a child a name" have often resulted in unhappy homes and divorces. Not wanting to marry does not make abortion necessary. There are other choices.

Overpopulation?

Some people, married or single, consider abortions because the world is already overpopulated. Why add to the problems? The population problem is real. If I thought of my children or your expected child as a future hungry mouth to feed, as a lifelong welfare case, I might also think about abortion. But if we think of your future child as a person loved by you and by God, as a person who gives to the resources of the world as well as takes, a person who adds to life; then abortion is not necessary. The difference between the two possible futures for your unborn child would depend on how the child is raised. If you feel the child is worthless and unwanted, then he or she will have little chance. But if the child is allowed to grow up in a home (yours or another) where it is loved, it can become a happy and valuable person.

Too Old?

Married women who find themselves pregnant when they think they are "old enough to know better" often consider an abortion. It is a shock to find that what was thought to be menopause turns out to be pregnancy. Such a woman may have her other children reared to an age she thinks will give her a little freedom for the first time in years. Her first reaction to the news is often, "Oh, no, not 12 more years of the PTA."

Concern for a woman's values in life and the effect of a baby on other children are factors that must be considered. Also, some older women have more difficulty in pregnancy, and there is an increased possibility of certain birth defects. But many older women have no more difficulties in pregnancy than their younger sisters—or their daughters. If that is the worry, see your doctor today.

The big problem of changing your mind set because you thought your family was complete is more difficult to solve.

The fact is, many families report that the "tag along" child has been a source of joy for everyone. Parents find themselves "young again" as they share the fun things the baby does with other, and younger, new parents. Older brothers and sisters get a little experience in child raising plus a built-in attention getter and giver. Also, that late child can grow up with a kind of leisure and security that few other children have. That's an ideal picture, and maybe it doesn't happen every time. But it can. Your attitude about yourself and the child will make the difference.

What's Important to You?

Perhaps most women face the possibility of an abortion with a "not now but later" attitude. They want to finish their education or help husband finish his. They want to get out of an apartment into their own home, or achieve a certain financial security before taking maternity leave. Or maybe it's a trip to Europe that's planned.

All of these are good and wonderful things. But then to many people having a baby is a good and wonderful thing. And sometimes having one means giving up the other.

Each person has to establish his or her own priorities. But when you are married, your priorities must be established together. If you had agreed to delay pregnancy for a set time but something happened, don't blame each other. Instead look again at what you want out of life.

Don't wait to have a baby until you can afford it. If everyone did, there would be an underpopulation problem. I'm in favor of good financial planning, and that means family planning many times. But a baby isn't a financial investment. Nor is it a luxury item. A baby is a part of you. There is no comparison between the joys of parenthood and other successes or achievements in life. That's a personal opinion, but I assure you it includes full knowledge that children can also cause frustration and disappointment. If you want one eventually, evaluate the reasons you are using for delaying having a child. Maybe there is no reason to delay.

If you do want children in the future, also consider something else. You may not be able to have more children. In this day of available birth control methods you may assume that all couples not having children are preventing conception. Not so. Many couples who conceive one child are not able to conceive again. I have known women who felt that they couldn't have children because God was punishing them for a previous abortion. If you have that kind of view about God, face it now, not later. Long ago I realized that if God treated me the way I deserved, nothing good would happen to me. But through Christ God treats us by grace, not justice. His love does not give permission for an abortion. But it does ask you to face now what your attitude would be if after an abortion you could not conceive again.

Afraid of Parenthood?

Maybe the idea of having a child frightens you. You don't know if you'll be a good mother. You wonder if your husband will love you in the same way if you have a child—though I'm afraid that men are more jealous of the attention their children receive from their wives, than the other way around. You may have bad images of young mothers whose figures have gone to pot, who wear housecoats all day, and who talk baby talk. It does happen that way for some. But it doesn't have to happen to you. Women who are good mothers also have identities other than "Mommy." They can still be involved in social and community activities. They can still hold down interesting and worthwhile jobs.

But You Are You

None of these reasons for considering an abortion describe your situation exactly. It is because you are an individual in your own set of circumstances that you have to make the decision on this matter. But it is important for you to know that others have been in similar situations. Some in your situation have decided to end the pregnancy. Other have had the child. Not all who made one choice are happy about it.

Nor are all of those who made the other choice miserable about it. But those who have the most trouble (no matter which decision they made) are those who considered only the moment, not the result of their decision.

Please take time to consider all the options before you.

CHAPTER 3
A Problem with the Problem

Like most problems the situation of a possible abortion seldom exists alone. Other conflicts, other guilts, other fears may add to the frustrations you now have. The idea, "Face one problem at a time," probably makes good sense to you right now. There is no way to solve all conflicts at once. And the question of abortion demands an answer right now. So it gets first priority.

Is Sex a Problem?

However, I would like to put another concern on the agenda for consideration now—that is sex. Maybe it is not wise to treat sex as a difficult situation. The subject, by itself and as it should be, is not a problem. It is much easier to discuss sex from the view of its joys and purposes in our lives. But it must be admitted that sex, like all good things, can become a problem. No book, let along one chapter of a book, can deal with all phases of one of the most complicated parts of human life. But we must consider sex as related to the present situation.

An authority on the subject has said that every person considering an abortion has a sex problem. According to that theory all people, including men, who are involved in a pregnancy that they want to terminate have a maladjusted sex life. I would agree only in light of the fact that a good medical examination could find something physically wrong with all of us. And a complete examination of our sex lives undoubtedly would find something out of whack in all of us.

Is Sex the Problem?

Our concern now is not to probe deep into your sexual training and experience. Rather it is to say that the situation of a possible abortion cannot be considered without also recognizing and examining your attitudes about sex. This is necessary for two reasons.

First, if you do have problems about sex, they may be related to your worries about your present pregnancy. If you understood the sexual part of the problem, you might be in a better position to make a decision regarding your pregnancy. Married or not, it is highly probable that tensions in the relationship with the man with whom you conceived are also reasons why you are considering an abortion. There may be exceptions to this, but you should at least examine your relationship with him. We'll go into detail on this subject in the next chapter. To deal only with the issues of an abortion without considering the sexual relationship is to ignore part of the facts that should influence your decision. If you leave out part of the evidence, the solution you reach will not apply to all of your life, but only to the part you evaluated. So it's better to consider the entire issue now and try to reach a decision that will fit into your total life.

Another reason you should consider your concepts of sex as you face a decision regarding a termination of pregnancy is for your own future. Your decision—not only to abort or not to abort but the reasons you do either—will have a great influence on your future sex life. Sex is an important part of your life. It cannot be denied, turned off, or ignored without hurting other parts of your life. It is part of the way God made you and is important in your relationship with people.

Going through an abortion, giving up a newborn child, or raising a child that you did not want, could make you afraid of sexual relations. Because you responded to the love and tenderness of a man you are now pregnant. Because you allowed your desire for sex to be fulfilled, you now face an important and far-reaching decision. If you are hurt by the results of that decision, you may either consciously or subconsciously reject a future sexual relationship.

Look to the Past and the Future

To avoid destroying your future sex life, you need to face the issues of your past sexual relationship. There may have been guilt involved. But guilt can be removed. I would be afraid to face with you the issues of a possible abortion and the possible guilt of your sexual relationship if I did not know that Christ removed my own guilt and did not believe that He did the same for you. In chapter 6 we'll go into detail about God's involvement in your life, but for now remember that guilt is a moral debt. Like financial debts, moral debts cannot be put aside with the hope that they will go away. The bills keep coming until they are paid. You need assurance now that any guilt involved with your situation is paid. And do not feel you are paying the price by the shame and pain you may now face. Abortion, with its surgical procedures and possible social castigation, must not be regarded as the sacrifice by which you pay for the guilt that accompanied pregnancy. Nor does giving up a child or raising an unwanted child pay the price. Christ has paid the price for you.

"Repentance is good for the soul." Everyone says it. And it's true—if the repentance is followed by an assurance that you are forgiven. My great concern for you now is that you do not add guilt to the problems you already face. Realize that if you don't connect your unwanted pregnancy with your sex life, those same problems may continue to give you dif-ficulties in your future. You do not have to overcome a negative score to start out even again. You can have a happy marriage with a satisfying sexual relationship.

Some women may react to the multiple-choice ex-perience of abortion, giving up a child, or raising an unwanted child, by becoming afraid of sex and a future relationship. Others may have the opposite reaction. For some unfair reason our society has made "getting caught" a greater sin than a sexual relationship outside of marriage. Part of the problem of an abortion for an unmarried person is the cover-up—keeping friends and relatives from knowing that the pregnancy ever started. If the pregnancy becomes public knowledge, some women feel they are branded for life. Like Hester Prynne they must wear a large psychological "A." (In Hawthorne's *The Scarlet Letter* a woman guilty of adultery was forced to wear an "A" for adultery embroidered on her dress to show her sin to all.) Such an attitude about guilt can lead to a feeling of worthlessness that says, "I am no good. Since I have done wrong, no one will want me for an honest sexual relationship."

For some women the abortion decision (no matter which way they decided) has been the banana peel that caused them to slide into a life of sexual promiscuity and frustration. Some have said to themselves, again either consciously or subconsciously, "I'm nothing but a whore; no one would want to marry me now." But that attitude is not only destructive, it is wrong. Many women who have dealt with an unwanted pregnancy later had happy marriages or full, meaningful, and moral lives without marriage. Your future sex life need not be destroyed by problems about sex that led to the present situation.

Emotional Amputation Not Necessary

Sex is much more a part of our emotional lives than our physical lives. Even though sex is expressed physically, the physical union must be based on deeper psychological and spiritual feelings to have meaning and purpose. When facing a problem regarding sex, it cannot be handled only on the physical level—by either avoiding the physical contact of sex or by going to the other extreme of having physical sex indiscriminately. Instead, total sexuality must be considered.

Look at it this way: If you had a disease in your arm, you could do one of two things—either treat the disease or amputate the arm. The faster method would be amputation. By one act you would be rid of the problem. But that solution

38

would cost you your arm. Treatment of the disease might be more painful and take longer, but you might regain use of the arm.

When a person has a sexual problem, it must be faced spiritually and psychologically. You must honestly examine your sexual feelings, training, and experience. You must be able to face the fact that in some areas you have been wrong and must know that you can change your attitudes and practices regarding sex. But such an evaluation of your own life is painful and takes time. Sometimes it seems easier to have an amputation, to cut off the emotional experience of sex, to remove it from your life. You can do that by either pretending there is no sex and saying you'll have nothing to do with sex again. Or you can do it by making sex a purely physical function—a physical release from tension that you need and that someone else needs, so why not do it and get it over with. But that attitude is an emotional amputation. It cuts the psychological and spiritual values of sex out of your life. It removes sex as a way to develop a close and lasting personal relationship involving not only the act of sexual intercourse but a life of touching, sharing, caring, and being together.

I am asking you not to have an emotional amputation regarding your sexuality. This request asks you to endure some pain now. Do not put more pain on yourself than you can take, and do not face the pain alone. Go to your pastor, a parent, or someone who understands and cares about you. Maybe you could just go through this chapter with another person. The effort will not sidetrack you from your decision regarding an abortion. It will help you consider the total problem and look for a solution rather than a way out. It will help you put things together in a way that will lead you back to a complete and full life rather than into further problems.

"Doing Sex" or "Being Sex"

To help you consider your past and future sexual experience it would help for you to think about how you

39

define sex. What is sex? There are different answers because people look at the question from different points of view. Naturally, a person's conclusions are determined by his or her point of view.

Some define sex as the act of sexual intercourse. From that view the action is described as having sex. The emphasis is only on the moments of physical contact. Sexuality boils down to a single function. Physically speaking, a man and woman who have never seen each other before and will never see each other again could be together for five minutes, have sexual intercourse, and produce a child. They have done sex.

The sex-as-activity view directs all attention to the moment when conception could occur if not prevented. In your situation of being pregnant and not wanting to be, this view of sex presents several questions. Which event caused the pregnancy? What happened to the birth control (if used) that time? What could have been done to avoid the problem I now have? Answering those questions might help you understand one part of the problem and give you ways to avoid future unwanted pregnancies. But I personally hope you gain more from your present situation than that. The "sex as something you do" view limits sex to a part-time and limited portion of your existence.

Another view of sex sees it as something you are, a part of your being human. Your sexuality is a part of who you are. It is something in and of you that relates to other people, both male and female. But it is also a special part of you that offers a unique relationship between you and another person. This special relationship includes "doing" sex, but it puts the action of sex in the setting of "being" sex. From this view sex is not a part-time experience, but is involved in all of your life. The wife is sexual not only in a bikini and in bed but also when her hair is in curlers and she is in a bathrobe that was rejected by the church's rummage sale. The man is sexual not only when he is athletic and powerful, but also when he belches and forgets to shave.

Maybe all of this sounds a little ideal and unreal. It does not mean that when husband and wife see each other in the less than attractive situations described above they immediately desire sexual intercourse with each other—though they might. But it means that a sexual relationship is more than sexual intercourse. A sexual relationship continues even when the partners are temporarily separated. It continues and grows during a time when sexual intercourse is impossible for physical reasons.

Sometimes this "sex as being" sounds a lot less exciting than "sex as doing." But the fact is that there is a lot more doing sex in a relationship built on being sexual than in those that are built only on the act of sex. I once picked up a hitchhiker who told me all about his interesting sex life based primarily on his hitchhiking. I'll admit his stories would make good copy for some popular magazines today, and if someone made a movie of his life, Burt Reynolds would get the lead. But it soon dawned on me that during that relatively short ride he was telling all of his sex experiences over the last several years. Living a "sex as being" life, I was glad I couldn't even remember last month's score of "sex as doing."

Check Your "Before and After" Sex Life

Maybe an example from the world of golf will illustrate the two views of sex in a way that will also help us in later chapters. (You don't have to be a golfer to understand this. I am not.) The direction and distance a golf ball goes is determined by the moment of impact between the club and the ball. The whole action occurs during the split second of impact. But it is what happens before and after that moment that determines the effectiveness of the hit. The golfer who wants to improve his game does not dwell only on the point of impact. That moment is too brief and too decisive to allow opportunity for evaluation and improvement. But the swing that goes before the impact and the follow-through that goes after can be controlled and improved. The effectiveness of the

41

actual impact can therefore be improved by developing a better swing and a better follow-through.

The meaning of the parable is this: Sex as doing is a point of impact. It is the moment of fulfillment in the relationship between a husband and wife. It is the time a child is conceived—in an act of shared love. But it is the swing and the follow-through that gives meaning and direction to the point of impact.

The swing and the follow-through as a part of sexuality can be seen both from an immediate and a long-range view.

The swing that prepares for a sexual life starts in childhood as a young person learns about sex from parents, classmates, and others. It develops through what adults unkindly call "puppy love," dating, serious courtship, to marriage. The attitude and experiences gained during that time of your life have an important bearing on the point of impact of your sexual experience now. You might feel that all of the growing up experiences are behind you now and it is too late to improve your swing. But not so. You can correct misinformation you received about sex. Feelings of guilt or inadequacy can be removed. You can change attitudes. Think about the experiences in your life that have influenced your views on sex today. Recognize those that may have caused you problems and do something to correct them. Find those attitudes that are wholesome and helpful, and develop them.

The swing that leads to the impact of sex also includes the approach to each sexual experience. It is not just the foreplay of sexual intercourse, but it is part of two people being together. It is saying "good-bye" in the morning in a way that indicates saying "good night" later on will be fun. It is kissing and touching even when sexual intercourse will not occur within the hour or even the day. It is investing in future sexual experiences together. It is appreciating the total relationship. A little extra time spent warming up is helpful for both golfers and lovers.

Apply this approach to the sexual experiences that led to your pregnancy. The point is not just whether sexual intercourse occurred before marriage. Even a husband and wife can fail to develop a sexual relationship based on total personness. In fact, it is a growing experience that starts in courtship, is not completed at the moment of marriage, but continues to develop for years. Did your sexual relationship have meaning beyond the moment of physical sharing? Was the goal of the relationship just to reach the point of impact or were there plans to follow through? Do you plan to offer each other more than just a physical experience?

In evaluating your preparation for sex, remember that your present action is preparing your future sex life. Look at the errors in your swing (your approach to sex) not just to expose guilt and mistakes but to receive forgiveness and correction.

Check Your Follow-Through

Now let's look at the follow-through of sex. A golfer dare not lose interest in his drive at the moment of impact. He must follow through because his plans to continue the swing after impact have an influence on the impact itself. What happens after a sexual experience is also important for you. You can do much to improve the actual sexual experience by working on your follow-through.

The most famous quote to survive the novel and movie *Love Story* is, "Love is never having to say you are sorry." As used in the plot I would argue the point. But the quote, by itself, can have a beautiful meaning. Unfortunately, people often have to be sorry about a sexual experience. The sex drive is so strong and overpowering that it makes people forget many other parts of life for the moment. Under the influence of strong sexual desire, we humans can rationalize numerous sexual experiences that we would otherwise avoid or even condemn. But after a sexual experience there can be a letdown or even a repulsion by what has happened. To have sexual intercourse and then say or feel, "I'm sorry," denies the meaning of sex. Love is never having to say you are sorry. It is enjoying not only the sex act but also the memory of it. It is having a follow-through that says, "We've got something good going here."

The follow-through of sex is not only the good feeling the next morning and something nice to daydream about at work the next day. It is also a life of sharing the total person you share sex with. "Going all the way" is rather a sad expression if it means all the way to a motel bed and no further. But "going all the way" is a beautiful thought if it means going all the way to share joys and frustrations, dreams and fears, failures and successes—the trip being via the altar, in my opinion.

Again, look at the follow-through of your sexual relationship that led to your pregnancy. I believe that it is possible for some people considering an abortion to have had a good sexual relationship. However, if that is true for you, it means the "you" refers not to "you, a woman" but to "you, a woman and a man." If you are facing this together, you have problems, but they are not as great as the woman who must decide alone.

In most cases the woman is left alone to consider or have an abortion. The follow-through is not what it should have been. If that is true in your case, recognize it now. It does not mean you are destroyed sexually. You can yet have a future, meaningful sexual relationship. But it does mean you need to see what went wrong the last time. Be aware of the responsibility of sex. Be willing to go all the way the next time. And make sure you are with a person who will go all the way with you.

CHAPTER 4
Who Else Is Involved?
—I: A Man

"It's My Body."

One of the most common reasons women use for an abortion is: "It's my body. I'll do what I want with it." If you stop to think about it, the statement is not an argument for abortion but rather it is a declaration affirming the right to make a decision about an abortion. After claiming her right to make decisions regarding her own body a woman could say either, "It is my body, and I choose to have the baby," or "It is my body, and I choose to have an abortion."

However, there are other implications in the it's-my-body point of view. Such a declaration of independence not only affirms the right to make one's own decision but it also establishes personal responsibility and an isolation from others.

If you have used the it's-my-body idea, I would like you to evaluate what you mean by it. You may have accepted it as a truism without considering exactly what you mean when you say it. All of us use commonly accepted sayings without thinking about their precise meaning. For example, I can accept both "Haste makes waste" and "Never put off until tomorrow what you can do today" even though they could contradict each other. They have to be applied to the right situation.

Because of the possible different interpretations I don't want to argue against the it's-my-body theory as a philosophy. Rather I would like you to consider some of the implications of the statement so you will be more clear about what you are accepting and what you are denying when you accept or reject the view.

"It's my body; I'll do what I want" could be interpreted in a way that few, if any, would agree with. Or it could be given a meaning with which most, if not all, people would agree. In this chapter and in the three that follow we are going to consider people who might feel they have some claim on you and therefore feel they have a responsibility for you. Maybe you do or do not want to declare your separation from them depending on how you view their involvement.

Is He Someone You Love?

First let's consider the man who shares with you the responsibility for your pregnancy. What does he have to say about a possible abortion?

Since this book is not intended to offer legal advice, we will not go into legal rights. Our concern is about a higher principle of life than the requirements of civil law. We want to consider the rights and responsibilities of each of you as you are related to each other. You need to understand your relationship prior to the beginning of the pregnancy, his present involvement with you, and what his relationship will be with you after the decision is made. Be very honest in your hopes for the future. Don't make your decision an effort to control the future.

Let's start by looking at an ideal situation. Suppose the man in question is your husband or your fiancé and, since this is the ideal situation, you have a good marriage or engagement. You love the man and trust him. You know he loves you.

In the ideal situation the it's-my-body theory seems unnecessary. You have given your body to the man, not just in the literal sense of sex, but in the spiritual and emotional sense of commitment. And he has given his body to you. He has placed your needs on an equal basis with his own. Because the two of you have established the kind of relationship into which a baby can be ideally born, you can act as a unit. You are united in a single channel of love. You qualify as parents because your sexual act was based on the love that is to provide for a newborn child.

Problems Are Still Real

Yet it is possible for a couple in an ideal situation to consider an abortion. They may have made plans for education, business, travel. There may be health problems. If they consider an abortion, they must be extremely sensitive to each other's feelings. It may be time to change plans, to rearrange schedules. Don't assume that the other partner does not want to change priorities. The birth of a baby may be more important than previously established goals. Above all don't think you know what the other person is thinking. Don't get in the situation where each is willing to give up the baby for the other when actually both want the baby.

Women facing a decision regarding an abortion under less favorable circumstances might consider the problem you face an easy one. If a man and woman have that much going for them, they could also adjust to the changes necessary to include a child. But the couple themselves make that adjustment. They can't do it on the basis that another person's problem is greater. However, they should be careful to look to their total life goals as well as the one's near at hand.

Now let's back off one step from the ideal. Suppose you are married but the relationship is a little shaky. Either you haven't established a good understanding and mutual trust, or other factors have caused problems in your marriage. Or you are engaged to be married, but have real doubts about the wisdom of getting married. One or both of you have talked about delaying the wedding date. Now you find yourself pregnant.

Now the it's-my-body concept has more meaning. If you do not have complete trust in the man and feel that his commitment to you has gaps in it, you may be including the possibility of a future without him. But you may also have a hope that the relationship will rekindle and there can be a future together. You already had problems to iron out. Now the possibility of either a baby or an abortion could complicate things.

Be aware of the causes of your dilemma. If you are only engaged, this situation illustrates a reason sexual intercourse belongs in marriage. Sexual attraction and desire are parts of a growing relationship between a man and woman. But the swing (preparation) must be completed before the point of impact. The possibility of getting pregnant before the relationship is well enough established to include a baby is one reason to reserve sexual intercourse for marriage. The delay is not out of fear of pregnancy (which can be prevented) but out of love and respect for each other. When two people are willing to share bodies, they are also willing to give up the it's-my-body view of life.

Since the situation already exists, make the best of it. Don't operate from guilt and shame or with the idea, "Since I've done one thing wrong, all that follows will be wrong." Realize that you are forgiven, and start putting things back together for a future solid relationship either with the man to whom you are now engaged or a person whom you have not yet met.

If you are already in a shaky marriage, your situation is more complicated. If a problem develops in marriage, you cannot avoid sexual relations until the conflict is resolved. The sexual relationship may help put the problem in proper perspective and get things going right again. On the other hand, it is unwise to plan a child when a marriage is in danger. This is one of a number of reasons to be grateful for satisfactory methods of birth control. But it's too late now to argue for a more careful use of them.

Also ask yourself why you got pregnant. Is it possible that you thought a pregnancy and a baby would keep your marriage or engagement intact? Was a baby a way to keep a man in line? Or look at the other side. Was it the man who threw caution to the wind and increased the chances of pregnancy? Was it a way for him to control you? Either man or woman can play that game.

But it's a dangerous game. Children are to be the product of a love relationship not a way to hold two people together. A husband and wife who stay together only because they feel a sense of obligation to children can be miserable and make the children miserable. A baby should not be a pawn used by parents to manipulate one another.

In raising these questions, I am not suggesting that it is unwise for you to have the baby. Rather I am saying that such situations are real—yours probably has some special implications—and that you must base your decision on the best possible understanding of the relationship between you and the man.

Is There Something to Build On?

Remember that it is possible for good to come from a less-than-good, or even a bad, situation. You can think of examples of babies born in shaky marriages, either before or after the proper nine-month test period, that grew up in normal, happy homes. And you can think of other examples in similar situations that had tragic ends. But counting up all the examples in an effort to establish the odds for a happy future for all of you won't help now. Instead, it is what you and your man are capable of doing that counts.

Could this big decision give both of you an opportunity to grow in your understanding of yourselves and of each other? Could it make you aware that you may need and can receive help from a counselor? Though neither the baby nor the pregnancy may ease the difficulty in your romantic relationship, the way you handle the problem could. You have an opportunity to show your willingness to cooperate with your lover. You can also make a new effort to accept his way of showing his concern for you. Remember, he can also improve.

Now is the time to improve your methods of communication—both speaking and hearing. Don't assume he knows how you feel. And don't assume you know how he feels. Find a way to communicate that helps you speak and him listen. Encourage him to do the same. Maybe it means you should put your thoughts in writing or on a cassette. Maybe you can talk better by phone, even if one of you has to go down to the corner pay phone. May you can talk to each other better if you have a third person present. Try it.

Though I pray that things can be worked out in your relationship with the man involved in your pregnancy, let's also include the possibility that all efforts fail. After an honest try, there still may be no way to have a future as a family. That does not mean you must get an abortion. It probably means you face a divorce or a broken engagement, but those are separate decisions from the issue of an abortion. You have other choices that will be discussed in chapter 8. Just don't let the decision about one part of the problem automatically decide other issues. Divide the total problem into as many categories as possible; then you can make the best decision for each part.

Being Pregnant Alone

Now let's consider another possibility. You are pregnant by a man with whom you know there is no future marriage. You don't want it. Or he doesn't want it. Or neither of you wants to get married. It is Marriage: Impossible.

In this situation the it's-my-body view probably makes the most sense—at least regarding the man involved. You never really gave him your body, and he never really gave you his. Each of you were only borrowing and loaning with no commitment.

One of the unfair facts of life is that the woman is left with the problems in this situation. That's the way it is, so we have to face it. It is unfair that she has to make the decision. She is the one who will miss work or classes while having either an abortion or a baby. She will feel the pain. She will even have

50

the financial burden unless he agrees to pay the abortion costs or child support. Either one can be a hassle, with threats of court action and the distaste of having to ask for the money.

It is also unfair in another way. This is from a man's point of view, but I think it should be included for a complete picture. It is unfair for a man to separate his sexual desire and satisfaction from the possibility and reality of children. Realize how many American men have left sons and daughters behind in Korea and Vietnam with no regard for their health, education, or spiritual life. From my point of view they have lost much of their sexuality by not having any "follow through" of their sexual experience. They have shown unawareness of a complete sexuality.

Maybe you, as a woman left pregnant by a man who feels no identity with the pregnancy, don't need to hear about his problems now. I remind you of it only to encourage you to develop a more complete understanding of your own sexuality now. You have been forced to face realities that he has avoided. By growing from this experience you will have more to offer a future relationship and you will be more capable of finding a man who better understands his total sex life. In the future you will look for a man who can offer you more than a sex thrill. And you will find a man who wants to give you more than that, but include that, too.

Do You Know Why?

Also ask yourself why you got pregnant under such circumstances. Not only why you had sexual intercourse, but also why you got pregnant when birth control methods are readily available.

Was the pregnancy really unplanned—unplanned in the sense that no efforts were made to prevent it. Pregnancies do occur even when birth control methods are used. But not often.

Did conception occur because one or both of you refused to use precautionary measures or were deliberately careless in their use? There are reasons why people take chances on getting pregnant.

Many men have responded to the announcement that their women were pregnant by saying, "Now I know I am a man. I'll pay for an abortion." It is unfair for a man to think that way, but it happens often enough to deserve further consideration. In the first place it is unfair for a man to use you to test his own masculinity. To put it crassly he has used you as a minor league to find out how he'll do in the major leagues. It is also an unreliable test. Manhood is not proved by the ability to reproduce.

Strangely enough, at least strange from the male perspective but maybe not to you, some women also react to pregnancy by saying, "Now I know I am a woman. I'll get an abortion." Do you think you had such a feeling either consciously or subconsciously?

It's natural for all of us to have concerns about our man- or womanhood. But often our efforts to prove ourselves create more doubts than give assurances. The real proof of our sexuality comes from a continued relationship. Tests are, by their nature, short lived and often create a fear of a permanent relationship.

Some casual relationships result in pregnancies because neither the man nor the woman wants to admit interest in physical sex only. She feels that if she is unmarried and on the pill, it makes her look available to any man who happens along. She would feel cheap; so she fools herself by refusing the pill and yet being sexually available. He feels that if he carries birth control devices it shows that all he wants is sex, and that's not a good line—at least not with most women. A man who has some respect, or wants to appear to have respect, for a woman also wants to appear interested in more than a trip to bed. So birth control methods are forgotten.

Are you honest with yourself? Do you feel that men are honest with you? Or do you play the little game "this is a meaningful relationship and we are not harming anyone" to excuse in yourself what you would condemn in others?

Another cause for pregnancies from casual relationships is a desire to get even with or control parents. Parents of girls, and many parents of boys, live under the threat of premarital pregnancy. Getting pregnant or making someone else pregnant is a way to rebel against parents and to get out from under their control. It is a game that makes everyone lose—like sinking the boat you are in to make another person in the boat wet. But it happens.

Another reason for unwanted pregnancy is ignorance. Ignorance not only about birth control but about sex itself. Even people who are highly educated in other areas can have a great lack of knowledge about sex. Don't be afraid to admit your ignorance and find out. Ask a person you trust for frank information. If you are reading this book, you can find others that give you good information about sex.

This list of possible reasons for pregnancy from casual relationships that offer no future is not complete. The point of mentioning these possibilities and encouraging you to consider your own situation thoroughly is to help you separate the problem of the pregnancy from the problem of the sexual relationship. Often the difficulties in that relationship are still there. Now you have an additional worry. Do not try to solve the second one, that is the pregnancy, while still fighting the battle of the first. Understand and accept whatever conditions led you to the place you are now. And find an answer to the concerns about the pregnancy that will also help in other problems rather than add to your difficulties.

Forgive and Be Forgiven

One final word about the man who is involved in your pregnancy. Forgive him.

Forgive him. That plea comes not just from me but from a person who has been through an abortion. No matter if he is a dear husband or a one-night boyfriend, he got you pregnant (if you say it that way, you might evaluate your own role in the conception) and you have problems. It will be easy for you to resent him and see him as the cause of your difficulties. Even if he is a husband you love, he will fail to understand all your feelings; and you can let resentment grow. If he is a married man who promised to divorce his wife but won't, or if he has disappeared, your hatred can grow and grow.

But you have enough problems without adding the problem of revenge now. No matter how wrong he has been, it will not help you to make him suffer. You will be right in requesting possible, but not impossible, financial help. But don't do it to make him hurt. You will not improve your moral image in the eyes of others by constantly telling how he was the one who caused the problem.

But most of all you need the assurance of forgiveness now. The forgiveness that helps is that which Christ gives out of grace, that He gives not because you deserve it but because He wants to help you. You cannot appreciate and find comfort in forgiveness unless you also permit the man involved to have the same forgiveness. Find a way to let him know you forgive even if he hasn't requested it.

He was involved in your becoming pregnant. Try to have him involved as much as possible in your decision regarding the pregnancy. Let him be involved in the forgiveness and hope that you now have for your future.

CHAPTER 5
Who Else Is Involved?
—II: Family and Friends

If the man involved in your pregnancy is being supportive and helpful as you make a decision about the termination or continuation of your pregnancy, you have help from the person who is in the best situation to give help. But the less involved he is and the less you want his help, the more you need the help of other people.

Who can and will be helpful to you depends on who you are and the relationships you already have with other people.

Who Are "They"?

The statement, "It's my body. I'll do what I please with it," is most often directed against society in general. It means that "they," people in general, have no right to tell you what to do. However, the "they" can become more specific. Many people will want to give you advice. You will resent some of it. Some of it might be judgmental and unfair. You may feel defensive in the presense of people who know about your dilemma. If they mention your problem, they appear to be interfering. If they ignore it, they appear not to care about you. But don't add to the conflicts you already have by erecting barriers between you and others with whom you live.

Those who make suggestions to you are those who feel they are somehow a part of your life. Most of them (allowing for the fact that there are a few bossy people around) do not want to manage your life. They want to show you that they are not rejecting you and they do care about you. Those who say nothing are trying to be tactful and show they want to continue a friendship with you. Don't expect all people to be sensitive to your exact needs. Some things people say may sound trite and simple; other things may sound condemning or hardhearted. People do sometimes say the wrong things for the right reason. Assume they mean well unless they clearly indicate otherwise. Most people will be looking for a way to show they care about you but do not want to interfere. They are looking for a way to say, "It may be your body, but we are a part of your life. We want to share in your life—including your present situation."

One of Satan's more sneaky and successful tricks is to make people think they are alone in a problem. If the Tempter can make you feel that others either don't care about you or are against you, he has isolated you from the greatest help God offers, that is other people. Most other people, especially those who are important to you, can understand your needs and will do their best to help you.

You will need the help and understanding of certain people. There will be others whose advice you will not want. You have to make the choice. Even the people you admire and respect will give you conflicting advice. Again, you will have to make the choice when it comes to a final decision. Do not look for people who will tell you what to do. If you follow their advice and later feel you did the wrong thing, you will blame them. Do not use well-intended advice as a cop-out for your own responsibility to select the facts that apply to you and to make your own decision. Others can serve you best by helping you understand yourself.

You may find that when you are suddenly faced with such an emotional decision as a possible abortion, you have a different attitude about people you have known for a long time. Those who had been close to you and with whom you had shared personal feelings may not be the most helpful ones now. On the other hand, those who had not been your most intimate friends may suddenly be the ones you feel can

56

help. If this happens, it does not mean you are throwing away old friends and making new ones. It could be you recognize that your present situation is temporary and that when life is back to normal you will want to keep the close friends without having the memory of the "big problem." Or it could be you realize that some people are not able to cope with the possibility of an abortion. Even though you still love them and know they would still love you, they are just not equipped to handle the emotional outlay such a situation requires. Other people by their natural instincts, personal experience, or professional training will be in a better position to give you the help you need.

You will have to let those who can help you, know that you need their help. Many will say, "Is there anything I can do?" Don't be afraid to say yes and tell them what you need. Also don't be afraid to say no and explain that you are receiving the kind of help you need but that you appreciate their concern.

You may feel you do not want anyone to know about your pregnancy. Especially if you think you may decide to have the abortion or give the baby up for adoption, it may seem that the fewer people who know about it the better. I agree; such information does not have to be published either officially or unofficially. And I hope you don't feel a need to tell everyone about your problem. But talking to others is not only a way to find your own answer, it is also a way to test the answer. Find out if you are willing to live with a decision before you go through the action. In the event you have an abortion, you will need physical, emotional, and spiritual help. Line it up now. If you keep the child, you will need many kinds of help, including maybe financial. Line it up.

You Have a Family

Take a look at some of the people who are most likely to help you. I'll suggest some categories. You fill in the names and rank the possibilities.

First consider your family: mother, father, sister,

brother. If you have a special family situation that gives a grandparent or a favorite aunt or uncle special status, insert them in the list.

Your first reaction may be that your family members are the last people you want to know about your pregnancy. And you may be right. But you may be wrong. Some parents have a far better ability to adjust to startling situations than their children think. Your family has had the most lasting relationship in the sense of time. You are right that they are the ones that may feel most hurt by your problem. But for that same reason they may be the ones most willing to help. If you can tell them and they can take it, they can help now. And their knowing will solve one thing for the future. You will not have to live with the fear that somehow they will find out. You will not have to wonder if you look strange each time the subject of abortion is mentioned when you are with them.

Your family has taught you your sense of morality. And whether you like it or not, your values are probably about the sames as theirs. Even though you may temporarily find yourself disagreeing with them, on the long haul your value system will probably be not much different than the one you learned from them. You should know what they think about abortion. How would they react to the idea of a grandchild being offered for adoption? Would they accept you and your child if you kept the baby? If some experiences have made your views different from theirs, can you explain them in such a way that their views might also be adjusted?

Remember that your parents taught you a standard of morality that they wanted you to follow, but they were aware that you would not be a perfect person. High moral standards are maintained not because we never break them, but because when we do break them we do not lower the standard to the level of our behavior. Instead we recognize our violation of the standard and try to return to it again.

Looking at the total picture of your present problem—that is including not just next week but also next year and the years that follow—it would be best if you were able to tell your family and ask for their help. There may be some yelling and crying or whatever else your family does to handle frustrations. But no matter how old you are, they still feel a responsibility for you. They still believe their lives are involved with yours and yours with theirs.

If there are reasons that make you sure you cannot tell your parents, do not blame them. Right now you are looking for help, not for excuses for not having help. If you decide they can't be involved, then they are not rejecting you but you are saying you do not need the kind of help they can give.

If you ask them for help and they give it, remember that they cannot make the decision for you. Each person who gives advice gives it according to his or her interest in you and according to the way your decision will affect their lives. Sometimes parents have suggested or demanded an abortion for their daughter to protect their own social standing in the community. Others may want you to have the baby and offer to take it in their home because they would like another child. While you must be concerned about your action's influence on them, you must remember that it also affects you the most. Perhaps one of the biggest helps you will get from telling your family is that you won't have to always guard what you say in the future and plan little lies to keep a cover-up going.

You Have Friends

Next, let's consider friends who might be in a position to help you both because they have the ability to help and because your relationship is such that you could accept help from them. Maybe you can turn to certain friends naturally without even thinking about it. You know they will help. But maybe you wonder if this problem would disrupt the friendship. Maybe they can't help. Let's look at a few possibilities.

For one thing you probably know people who have had abortions, others who have placed a child for adoption, and others who, though not married, have kept their own baby. Such people should qualify as experts. They speak from experience while most of us speak from theory. And talking to such a person may be helpful to you. But remember one thing—their advice will be based on their situation. And your situation may be different in many ways. Also those who have made such an important decision as described might feel a need to justify their own decision by encouraging you to do the same. That one woman got an abortion, gave up a baby, or reared a child alone is not a reason for you to do the same. Yet that person's experience can help you evaluate what would happen to you if you made the same decision.

Instead of asking for conclusions from a person who has faced the same situation, ask for a list of questions. From another person's experience you can establish your own priorities. Many times we make decisions by asking the wrong questions. If the other person tells you what questions were important in her decision and what questions she wishes she would have considered, she has been helpful to you.

Another friend may have the right contacts to recommend a person to do an abortion, a place to stay while having a baby, or an adoption agency. All that kind of information may be needed, but that is not necessary while you are trying to decide whether or not to continue the pregnancy. Don't make a decision only because the kind of help needed was that most readily available. There are reliable, honest professionals who will help you no matter which decision you make. Do not deal with back-alley abortionists or black-market adoption rings.

Friends who will be the most helpful to you are those who understand your needs. Listen to those who know when to let you cry and when to tell you to wipe your nose and get back to living. Listen to those who tell you not only what you want to hear but also what you should hear.

There Are Professionals

You might also want to consider a special kind of friend who could be helpful to you now. Would you like to talk to your pastor, doctor, lawyer, a former teacher, or counselor? It can be helpful to have counsel who knows you but is not emotionally wrapped up in your life or the lives of members of your family. Sometimes even a stranger can be a help, if you know the person is reliable and in a position to become involved. As a parish pastor I often had people unknown to me and not members of my denomination come to discuss personal problems such as abortion. Their coming to me didn't mean they wanted to join my church. They wanted to talk to someone about personal details, and they didn't want to take time to go through a long get-acquainted period. Frankly, they also wanted to talk to someone they could see regularly. That was fine with me. You might appreciate that kind of help now too.

A professional will be able to give you facts you need to know or information about where you can find out. You may want medical details about abortion. Don't be certain you know the details. Talk to a doctor and ask anything. Also understand the doctor's role. Any doctor will talk to you about an abortion, but some will not perform one. He or she is not rejecting you or your decision by refusing to terminate your pregnancy. The doctor also has a right to make his or her own decisions. It seems strange to me that some of the same people who have insisted that an individual has the right to decide whether or not she wants an abortion now insist that a doctor should be required to perform the operation. The freedom that allows you to evaluate your situation and reach a conclusion also gives another person the same privilege.

You should also know the legal facts and the procedure involved in an adoption. You may have heard of unusual or irregular adoption practices and assumed that all adoptions are handled in the same way. Find out.

A pastor can be helpful not only in reaching a decision regarding your pregnancy but also in keeping the rest of your life tied together. Talking with a pastor may present one of the same problems as dealing with parents—he has been an authority figure. He is the one who told you not to misuse sex and maybe that abortion is wrong. Therefore, to go to him for advice may seem like a contradiction. You have already ignored his advice. But the pastor does not only teach morality. He is always dealing with people, including himself, who have failed to live up to the ethical principles he teaches. He can help you accept your failures without losing your personal integrity.

One of my friends told me that as she considered an abortion she was afraid to go to the pastor because she remembered what he had taught in confirmation class— things she had not followed as taught. Later she had the opportunity to be with him and realized that he had also taught love and forgiveness in the confirmation class. Now she feels she could have discussed a possible abortion with him and he could have helped.

People in any of the helping professions can apply a wide range of experience and training to your situation. He or she will probably have worked with people who have had abortions and those who have refused abortions. They will be aware of the different circumstances that led to each decision. Rather than responding from only one view a counselor can help you see many options and let you rank them according to your values. But—need I remind you—professional people can have their individual hang-ups too. Even as you do. Recognize their biases and make allowances for them as you would with anyone else.

And There Are Others

Let's consider one more group that only vaguely comes under the category of family and friends—that is, people in general: the cousins, the family three doors down the street, former classmates, the in-law's in-laws, and other acquaintances.

We all care what people think about us—even total strangers. It hurts to know, or even think, that others are talking about us in a judgmental way. But we might as well admit that not all people will be understanding and supportive. Some will be critical behind your back or even to your face. There are those who will condemn you no matter what choice you make. It's not personal—they'd do the same for anyone. Also it's not permanent. They will soon lose interest in your "case" and find something more current.

But I urge you not to overreact to the few people who voice their criticism of you in a way that hurts rather than helps. Don't develop a thing against "nosy old men" or "gossipy old women." Don't feel threatened by people who have made decisions different than your own and insist on telling you about it—or the decision their sister-in-law's neighbor in Omaha made, and "her situation was exactly like yours." Don't condemn all people in a church or a community because one or several are insensitive and judgmental.

If you react strongly against any real or imagined criticism, you will build up a resentment that may eventually make you into the kind of super-critical person who is now giving you a rough time. One of the blessings you can take with you from this experience is a greater degree of tolerance. One of your problems has been, or may be, exposed to public scrutiny. But you have other faults and weaknesses that most people don't know about. We all do. You have survived with those faults, and you can survive whatever led to this problem. Don't try to defend yourself and explain your rightness to everyone. You will make it because you are forgiven, not because you have never done anything wrong. Apply the same understanding to others—also others who have faced different problems.

Life Goes On

We have rapidly gone through a long list of people who may help you. you may think of others. As you face this situation in your life, remember that you are still the same person you were six months ago. While the pregnancy and your concern about it demand most of your energy and time now, you still need relationships with people based on other areas of your life. Don't hide from the world. Continue to visit family and friends. Keep on going to church. Accept social invitations and invite others to share fun with you.

You may be with people who do not know and do not need to know about your problem. It can be a relief just to talk about movies and ball games again. You are more than a woman who is pregnant and not sure she wants a baby. You are a person. You need to keep your life in balance. You need to continue relationships with family and friends that will last long after the present crisis is over.

CHAPTER 6

Who Else Is Involved?
—III: God

One of the biggest problems with the it's-my-body theory is in relationship to God. Is it saying to God, "It's my life and I'll do what I please"? If so, the attitude asks for a spiritual amputation that deprives you of help now and could cause you difficulties in your future relationship with God. The first sin, when Adam and Eve ate the forbidden fruit, was not that they stole apples from God. Their sin was that they rejected God's claim on their lives. They said, in effect, "Look, God, if we like that fruit, we'll eat that fruit. You can't control our diet." For the sake of a between-meal snack they shoved God out of their lives. But they wanted to show they were independent. Most of our problems today can be traced to a similar attitude.

Go Away, God

When one of my children was slightly over three, he came into the kitchen where my wife was baking cookies. Naturally he asked for one. His mother told him that the cookies were for supper and he'd have to wait. So he stood there looking at and smelling freshly baked cookies.

"Mommy," he finally said, "would you go out of the kitchen?"

His intention was obvious. He planned to take a cookie and didn't want an authority figure to be a witness. You should consider the possibility that you feel the same way about God during your time of decision. You may be afraid that what you do will be against His wishes for you. Therefore, it would be better if He were not around when you did it. Even to pray is to remind God of your existence; so it might be better to keep quiet for a while in the hope that He won't notice what you do.

. I hope you have not felt a need to hide from God, but many people do when they are in a period of conflict. Some will try to deny the existence of God, arguing that if there is no God there is no one to judge their decisions. Others will find fault with God. Somehow or other He gets the responsibility for letting the situation exist. Of course, if you can pin the blame on Him, He can't blame you for doing something wrong. Both of these efforts to get God out of the decision tell God to go away for a while.

However, I urge you to keep God in on this decision-making session. You need Him now as you may have never needed Him before. One of the many good things that could come from this episode of your life is your discovering (if you don't already know) the joy of being loved by a good and gracious God.

Take a Look at God

But maybe you don't see the goodness of God now. God is so complex that no description or view of Him can be complete. No one grasps the totalness of God. You can see Him as a Lawgiver, a Judge, a Father, a Savior, a Creator, a Provider. You can think of Him as being near and personal or as distant and majestic. All the views are correct, but any view by itself is inadequate.

It is dangerous to select only one attribute of God and ignore the others. You might see Him only in the Lawgiver-Judge role. That view could make you afraid of Him. It might make you more aware of past and present guilt something you don't need now.

Another view of God that could be dangerous for you now is to see Him as a kindly old grandfather who shuts His eyes when you sin. Such a view starts on the truth that God is love, but it misunderstands love by seeing it as permissive. God's role is to help us and that help includes guidance for our lives. To love someone does not mean to approve of everything they do. God loves you in such a way that He is willing to risk offending you rather than letting you use His love as an excuse for doing what would hurt you.

Who Speaks for God?

One of the problems that prevents us from getting a good grasp on God is that no one can speak for Him with absolute authority on all subjects. He gives us a number of clear messages that we can pass on to others. I can tell you that He loves you and that He wants you with Him. The truth of that statement does not depend on me or my ability to communicate. It depends on what God has communicated to us by sending His Son, Jesus, to be a part of our lives and to do something about our problems.

But the problem comes when we get to the question period. After hearing of God's love and forgiveness, many of us (me included) would like to ask a few questions. Right now you might like to ask, "Is it okay for me to have an abortion?" Or, "What will happen to my baby if I give it up for adoption?" Or, "Will I be sorry if I try to raise this child by myself?"

But God hasn't given us the authority to speak for Him on details that are not clearly revealed to us. I assure you that I have no "hot line" to God that I can use to check up on His opinions on current issues. And no one else has such a private source of authority either.

It is dangerous for any of us to play God. We do it each time we start our reasoning with, "I can't imagine how God would . . ." That sentence can be completed by making God for or against abortion. But the point is that we can't imagine ourselves into God's position. We don't have the information, wisdom, or compassion available to Him. He shares those things with us, but our ability to use them is limited. His abilities have no limitations except those we impose by limiting His work through us. And that's a big limitation. Be careful about trying to pretend that God is on your side because yours seems more logical. And accept others' "I feel that God would . . ." views in the way they are given—as personal opinion, not divine statement.

He Speaks in His Word

The Bible does not say, "Thou shalt not commit abortion." But it doesn't say, "Thou shalt," either. It speaks of miscarriages caused by accidents, but the issue is carelessness rather than a desire not to have a baby. God does speak of life in the womb as being a person—a person planned by Him. And He also speaks of His plan for people not only before their birth but before they were conceived. We were all conceived in the mind of God before we were conceived in the wombs of our mothers.

When the Bible does not spell out the exact details on a given subject, we often try to help God make up His mind in one of two ways. Either we make exact what He left vague, or we ignore His advisory way of telling us something because He didn't hit us over the head with an absolute law.

Some want to make the commandment "Thou shalt not kill" also read, "Thou shalt not have an abortion." Bumper stickers in my part of the country proclaim, "Abortion is murder." I agree that abortion can be murder, and my life would be easier (as long as I never got pregnant) if everyone accepted an absolute position against abortion.

But most people, though not all, see some exceptions. The official proclamations of most church bodies that are against abortion in general have allowed the possibility of certain pregnancies being terminated. Most of the official approvals of abortion are those we are not considering in this book— pregnancies resulting from incest, rape; a young girl's pregnancy, a situation that would cause the mother's death.

Such special situations dare not be used to show that all abortions are acceptable. An exception does not disprove a law. Situation ethics are unethical when you apply the conclusions from one situation to a different set of circumstances.

Are There Choices?

Yet the fact that some abortions are regarded as moral, also admits there is room for human judgment. Who has the right to make such decisions? There must always be borderline cases. It is easy to find an example at either extreme—one that everyone would agree has a right to an abortion and another that would have no right to an abortion. But who establishes the breaking point between these two positions? There will always be situations where an abortion would be approved by one group of people but condemned by others.

Morality is not established by majority vote or by popular opinion. The increase in abortions performed today does not make abortions morally right. Nor do liberal abortion laws mean that abortions are declared right by God. The new laws merely say that it is the individual's sense of morality rather than society's that must make the decision. To make and enforce laws that bind people to a procedure allowing no room for human consideration and personal judgments can harm, if not destory, the value of life.

On the other hand, I hasten to add, the lack of laws to guide people can also destory the value of life. To use an argument from silence: "God didn't tell us in clear words not to have abortions; so we can . . ." is unfair. If there were no laws or concerns about abortions, extreme acts to terminate pregnancies might occur.

Even people who advocate liberal abortion laws require that the abortion be completed in the first trimester (three months) of the pregnancy. While some would approve an abortion for almost any reason during the early part of pregnancy, most would be opposed to terminating a pregnancy in the sixth month. It could be argued that an abortion that is moral one week is also acceptable the next week, the next day, and so on. One person made the suggestion (though I

69

must assume he intended it to show the difficulty of establishing time limits on such things) that a law be passed that a human being comes into existence two days after its birth. In that way all who were born physically or mentally deformed could be eliminated before their official existence.

I hope you can operate between the two extremes "no abortion for any reason" and "any abortion for no reason." For the sake of society in general I hope that neither side "wins" so that we have either no abortions or an open abortion policy. All the attention that has been given to abortion reform laws by both proabortion people and prolife groups have made the issue public. Now parents, churches, and schools must give attention to the subject. Now children will need to be taught a life value that includes views on abortion. The open forums of the public media will have to present the issues so that people can evaluate them and come to a conclusion about abortion before the matter is of personal concern to them.

It is doubtful that you had much training about the subject of abortion during your childhood. So you're getting a crash course now. Don't resent, and don't be frightened by, the extreme statements made by those who are arguing for or against abortion. Apparently it is necessary to have people speak for far-out positions on most subjects to get the public aware of the issues and reach conclusions that are moderate.

Want To? Have To?

But to find God's direction for you now, I think we need to look in another direction. God does not make laws just to control the outward part of our behavior. Working under laws, people become technical: You can have an abortion for this reason but not for that reason; an abortion is okay today but would be immoral tomorrow. But God's direction is more concerned about our motives than technical obedience or disobedience. He prefers to change our hearts and let our hearts change our lives. People can always find a way to wiggle around laws through loopholes or their own creative exceptions. But God's method of guiding us by His love asks us to use that love in our decisions, puts a new light on our methods of reaching a conclusion. You can decide this question assured that God loves you and wants to help you. He is not playing guessing games with you in a way that you must be afraid to make a choice because you might displease Him.

Look at it this way: God does not give us any laws just to test our willingness to obey Him or to make us do something that will be only for His advantage. Every moral law is for our good and good for Him only in the sense that He loves us and wants what is best for us. His laws are to protect us—to protect us from ourselves and from others. When you obey any of God's laws, you are doing yourself a favor, not Him.

We obey God's laws most of the time because His way is the best way. But there are times when either the choice is unclear or His way seems to be the one that causes us more problems. Our conflict with God is that He sees our total life, all parts of it and for all times; we tend to look at only one part of life and only at the present. But when we make decisions on limited bases, the solution for one part of life can cause problems for other parts. The easiest course of action today creates new problems for the next day and the following year. God's way is to see the total picture and lead us through areas that may be difficult now but good for the future. He has a better future planned, not only in heaven but also here on earth.

It takes faith to follow God's advice during times of difficulty—faith to understand what is His way and faith that He will be with you. That faith is more than knowing He is right. It is a trust in Him—a trust based on the track record He established as a loving and gracious God by sending Christ to be our Savior. God has gone to the extreme of sacrificing His Son for you. With that kind of love for you shown by a death and a resurrection for you, you can trust that He also wants to help you now. He forgives you when you are wrong and helps you avoid wrong by directing your life to good. When you

71

follow His will you are not doing Him a favor; you are accepting help from Him. Don't make your decision regarding an abortion with the idea of earning His goodwill. You have His goodwill; therefore you can make the decision.

Will God Let You Know?

But how will God let you know exactly what you should do. If only He would come through with a clear and final answer. Right now you might agree with the wiseacre remark, "Only God knows and He's not telling."

Don't dump your decision on God in the wrong way by flipping a coin and praying, "Lord, tell me what to do. Heads I get an abortion; tails I don't." One of the dangers of asking God for a sign is that if the first toss doesn't go your way, you may pray, "How about two out of three?" The bigger problem is that such a prayer is a cop-out. By putting the decision on God you have a way to blame God for everything that goes wrong after the decision is made. And you fail to grow as a person.

Instead, see that God is with you. See His love for you as He has shown it in Christ. Jesus spent His life with people who were wrong. He was never afraid to tell them about their wrong, but He also offered forgiveness and a new way of life. You are not standing at a crossroads, with all that is good in one direction and all that is evil in another. There will be both joy and sorrow, guilt and grace either way you go. As sinful people we cannot always choose good and reject evil in our daily decisions. There will always be some wrong involved in our choices—either in what we choose or in our reason for making the choice. But because Christ is with us, there will also be good. His goodness becomes real in our lives. Hang on to that good part. Think about not only your own needs but the needs of others. Look at the love He gives you and give that love to all others affected by your decision.

And pray. And pray.

Pray not only for guidance in your decision but also for the ability to understand His will and the strength to follow it.

72

It is a relief to know that you can talk to God in bold, honest language because He already knows everything about you. You can tell Him about your sex life, your doubts, the desperate feelings you may have had. But He won't be shocked. He knew those things about you before He told you He loved you. He knew you needed help; so He came to you as your Savior. When you tell Him about a problem, you are not telling Him something new; you are telling Him you will accept His help.

One Christian women told me she could never have survived an abortion had she not remembered a Bible verse from confirmation days, "I can do all things through Jesus Christ who strengthens me." Another told how as she waited for an abortion with another woman there for the same purpose, the other asked, "Will God forgive us for this?" They discussed God's love and grace in the moments before their abortions.

Neither of these women claimed that God put His seal of approval on their abortions. But they were saying they felt His love and help for them. Most of us have learned to live with the fact that God can love us while we are sinners. We struggle with our everyday sins of selfishness, pride, prejudice, swearing, and the like, knowing they are not right yet knowing that God will not reject us because of them. We know his love does not approve of our action. But we often have difficulties applying His love. In something like abortion a person must decide on the action and make plans to follow through. But God's love is great enough to overcome our ideas about the relative seriousness of sinful acts. He forgives.

It is true that repentance is necessary to receive the blessings of Christ's forgiveness. But repentance does not earn the forgiveness—it realizes the need and seeks forgiveness. Christ does both the earning and the giving. Do not shut your eyes to God now and quickly go through an abortion with plans to repent later. You may be able to honestly repent later, but the tactic of shutting God out while you do something that either is or might be wrong could become a habit. You might decide to throw a few other items on the list before you have a big moment of repentance.

Do your repenting now. Clear out all old problems, especially any concerning the sexual relationship that started the pregnancy. The assurance of God's love and forgiveness, the promise of His continued help, and the power of His life in yours may make you decide not to have an abortion. God's grace has spoken. You may still not see a way out other than through an abortion. Your repentance is for the situation you are in as well as the acts you do. Keep God's mercy before you. Recognize the help He wants to give you. Use it. And pray.

The Dilemma We Share

I know you are in a dilemma as you face this moral issue. By wanting to share in your problem I have put myself in a dilemma too. Let me tell you about the confusion I feel.

I don't want to tell you, "An abortion is wrong, but do it anyway and God will forgive you." If it is wrong, then it is a wrong against yourself and others and you should not have an abortion. Nor do I want to tell you that it might be right for you to have an abortion. If you have an abortion on the basis that you are right, then you are saying you do not need God's forgiveness. And the sureness of that forgiveness is the one thing that makes me willing to face your situation with you.

Your comfort in this situation cannot be based on the fact that you have made the right decision. Your comfort must come from Christ's rightness, not yours. Your responsibility, living in Christ's rightness, is to make the better choice of those open to you. Face the possibility that you might be wrong. You have been before. When you know you have been wrong and were not destroyed, you don't get in a position of having to defend yourself. Don't live the rest of your life trying to justify the decision you make.

There are still other factors to be considered—the next chapter is important. Right now I want you to be, and I pray you see yourself, in the hands of a merciful God. You can do all things through Christ Jesus, who strengthens you.

74

CHAPTER 7

Who Else Is Involved?
—IV: A Baby? A Fetus?

In each of the last three chapters we have considered others who are involved in your life and therefore have an interest in your decision to continue or to terminate your pregnancy. In each case one of the problems was communication. How are you able to express your feelings and needs to others? How are they able to show their feelings and help for you?

A Problem of Words

This chapter will be the most difficult because it has an even bigger communication problem. It is about your unborn, or yet nonexisting, child with whom there can be no communication. Even the choice of words is difficult in our communication because the words selected already indicate a point of view.

Is there a baby involved in this decision? Or is there a future baby that might come into existence depending on your decision?

How do you think of and speak about the cells in your womb? Is it a part of you in the same sense as your appendix? Does the it's-my-body theory apply also to that which is evidence of your pregnancy? Would its removal be only an operation that takes out part of your body tissue? Or is it already a separate human life?

Medically speaking, those living cells are called a fetus. The question is: Is a fetus another state of human life similar to the categories baby, child, adolescent, and adult? Or is it a term for prehuman existence, such as male sperm or female egg?

There are no simple answers to such questions. The many answers given conflict with one another because each is given from a different point of view. The different answers may each be correct from their own perspective. The questions for you are: Which answers would I have given before I was aware of this pregnancy? What answers do I accept as true now? What answers will I believe a year from now? Five years from now?

Your view about the humanness of the fetus will ultimately have the greatest influence on your decision about an abortion. If you believe the fetus is now a human being, then it is not only a child, but it is your child. If you believe the fetus is prehuman, then you will feel rushed to make a decision because, if you should decide to have an abortion, it must be done before you believe the life in you has become a person.

A Legal Person

Let's consider several different views of prenatal life. Offering these options does not mean that this is a multiple-choice question and everyone can make up her or his mind. But it does mean that you should not select one view because it happens to match your opinion at the moment. Later you will have to live with other ideas. It is better for you to consider a wide range of opinions now while you still have choices to make.

Legally, there seem to be contradictions about the status of a human fetus. Many countries, including Japan and Sweden, have long had laws that allow abortions for many reasons during the first three months of a pregnancy. Many states in the U.S. have adopted similar abortion laws. The Supreme Court has upheld the state laws and expanded the possibility for more readily available abortions anywhere in the country. The prolife movement today is not fighting as much against abortion as a surgical procedure as they are trying to establish the legal rights of an unborn child. Unborn children have the legal right to identification with their fathers even though he died shortly after their conception. Recently the legal rights of unborn children have been recognized in court cases involving damage suits.

The legal problem is: Who speaks for an unborn child. If their parents do not stand up for their rights under the law, who can? If parents mistreat or abuse a child, a court may make them change their behavior or take the child from them. Can a court force a woman to continue a pregnancy against her will? Now courts are saying no, not in the first three months of pregnancy. After that they can.

A Medical Person

Medical opinions are probably more important to you than legal views. When do medical doctors believe a child comes into existence? Obviously there are many answers to that question. Reliable, conscientious medical people are on both sides of the abortion issue. Some always see the needs of the woman, their patient, first and are more open to abortion. Others see the needs of the fetus, the patient with no method of communication, and are less inclined to approve an abortion. Many struggle through each situation with a great awareness that they cannot make such decisions and be right every time.

Medically speaking, there are a number of points in human development that could be regarded as the beginning of life.

In the early days it was assumed that human life existed in the male sperm and the female egg. By following that logic any method of birth control was regarded as sinful because it was murder. When it was discovered that women produce hundreds of eggs and men produce billions of sperm, the idea that each egg contained "a little girl" and each sperm "a little boy" was discarded. Only a merger of the two was regarded as the beginning of a new life.

Conception, the union of the sperm and egg, is an obvious act to regard as the beginning of life. It combines the life-giving genes of male and female. It happens at a measurable moment—and that satisfies the human need "to see to believe." However, sperm and eggs often merge without resulting in a pregnancy. If the fertilized egg does not become implanted in the wall of the uterus, the merged sperm and egg are discharged from the woman without her being aware that the union took place. The IUD birth control method does not prevent conception, but it prevents implantation. Therefore, some medical people accept implantation as the beginning of pregnancy and the beginning of a new life.

Quickening, the moment when the woman first feels movement in her womb, has been regarded as the beginning of life by others. Described from the outside point of view it seems the baby "wakes up" at that moment and starts to exist. Of course, from the fetus' point of view there was always movement, but the fetus was too small and the movement too slight for the woman to detect it.

The point of viability is regarded by many as the beginning of a new life. Medically speaking, viability is the time when the fetus could survive by itself outside the womb. But that is a difficult moment to establish because "by itself" can never be adequately defined. In the broad sense, no person is viable in that he or she can survive without the help of others. It is my habit to hide from the rest of the world while I work on manuscripts such as this one. Only a few days away from people prove to me that I could not live alone. Bluntly—I'd go nuts.

Even in a narrower sense, viability is difficult to establish. Many, if not most, newborn babies would perish if they were not given attention immediately after they are born. Extraordinary measures are used to protect the lives of premature babies and those born with medical problems. They were not viable. On the other hand, some fetuses expelled from the uterus by abortion have survived. Others have been "born" alive from an abortion and were allowed to die. They were as viable as a premature baby.

The viability concept is the one most commonly used today to establish the beginning of a human life; so it must be reckoned with. The idea works better as a philosophy than a fact. Yet it is often used as a fact to determine when an abortion is permissible.

Of course, we measure a person's life from the date of birth. Your birth date determined when you could start school, vote, and when you can retire. However, the advent of the Cesarean section and induced labor for childbirth have made the date of birth an arbitrary figure. And obviously, unborn babies do a lot of human things, such as suck their thumbs and morning push-ups. Knowledge about life in the womb makes birth a part of the human experience rather than its beginning.

A few people think of a baby as an "it" even after its birth. Some feel a baby is born only as a thing and that it becomes human as it gains knowledge and emotion. As one who has experienced the birth of three children I cannot understand that way of thinking. Moreover, even those who do accept that thinking would never be in favor of killing a child before it "became human" in their eyes.

Medical science does not give an exact answer to the question of the beginning of human life. It is not a failure of a profession. Rather it indicates the answer is beyond their range of responsibility. It is to the profession's credit that most medical people accept the values of the people with whom they work and try to give dignity to all human life.

A Psychological Person

The field of psychology has no need to establish a point in time that human life begins—except when dealing with a person who has mental or emotional problems related to a miscarriage or an abortion. Then they seek understanding for the person involved rather than an authoritive answer.

But your own psychological feelings about the human life

of a fetus are important. Remember that your present feelings must be considered along with your past and future views. You should not violate your total life style during an emergency situation.

Most young people can speak about their own children long before those children exist. A small child can say to its parents, "When I have kids . . ." Psychologically, the child has already accepted future offspring. Dating and engaged couples talk about their future children. They decide how many they will have and express their hopes for boys and girls. From an emotional point of view many children are conceived first "in the gleam of an eye"—the feeling of love and hope that is shared between a man and woman. Many couples give names to future children before or during pregnancy.

Evaluate your own mental and emotional attitude about the life in your womb. The fact that you may not be filled with love and excitement about a prospective baby does not mean you don't accept the fetus as a child. Resentment against a possible baby may be against circumstances the baby will change rather than the baby itself. Speaking for most parents (at least the honest ones) I can admit that I sometimes resent and have other negative feelings about my three. But they are very real to me, and I love them dearly.

The next question is sharp and must be considered as a probe, not an accusation. Some parents become so angry at or frustrated with their children that they abuse them physically or.kill them. Will you later, if you decide on an abortion, regard your act in that light? Will you think of it in terms of having prevented or ended a life?

There can be psychological scars following an abortion. One of the chief purposes of this book is to encourage you to be honest with yourself and evaluate your feelings before you make a decision. If thinking about some of these things has only deepened your anxiety and made you more confused, please find a counselor to talk to now. Don't wait until later.

A Spiritual Person

We considered many of the spiritual aspects of an abortion in the previous chapter. There is one point that should be added to give a spiritual view of a fetus.

In case you haven't heard of the word "ensoul," let me introduce you to it. Ensoul means to endow with a soul, it describes the act by which physical life becomes also a spiritual life. Many of the moments discussed earlier as the beginning of a medical life have also been called the moment of ensouling.

One view of the beginning of a new life is that God creates each new person through physical methods and then creates a new soul for that body. God would ensoul a body. This view involves God in a new act of creation each time a child is conceived, born, or whenever the ensouling occurs.

Another view is that the birth of a child is an act of God's continuing creation. In the second view a child is a continuation of the parents' lives rather than a new creation. In this way of thinking God gave His original creation a way to share in His activity and keep the creation going by reproducing its own kind.

You don't have to choose between the two views, because there isn't that much difference between them. But the two views can help understand the abortion situation. The idea of a new creation for each birth demands a moment of ensouling—a moment that we cannot pinpoint with authority. Theologians are divided on this issue. Some are sure they know the answer, but to accept their answer one must accept the face which they base it. Theologians, like medical authorities, must sometimes admit that answers to some questions are beyond their professional range.

However, understanding the birth of a child as a part of God's continuing creation does not require a moment of ensouling. The act of passing life from generation to generation is not just through a sex act followed by a new creation. The "swing, impact, and follow-through" (from

81

chapter 3) are all a part of the continuation of life. The beginning of a new life is not just a moment in history but is a spin-off of the continuing life cycle. A small child is already involved in the process of becoming a parent as he or she grows up aware of sexual roles and responsibilities. A man and woman participate in the production of a new person, but their act in continuing creation is not just a sexual relationship that conceives a child. That is a continuation of their early relationship, and their involvement continues during the follow-through of their act of physical love as they continue to share love with one another and the child. During the development of a new life there are many great moments—all important for the continuing life cycle. The act of creation is not just, "We're pregnant!" but also, "The baby's here." She's growing up." "He's getting married." Also the everyday activities of children who become parents and produce children who become parents . . . are part of the way God continues His creation.

This continuing view of God's creation is not intended as an argument for or against abortion; though it can be used for either. It speaks against abortion in the sense that God's life is always considered to be a part of the growing new life in a woman's womb. It could never be destroyed. On the other hand, if there were a necessary reason for an abortion, this view would help the parents understand that a life is not being destroyed. That life is still only a branch of their lives. Though the growing part of their mutual life might have to be stopped, the source of that life would continue in the parents and their present or future children.

The spiritual view of a person always includes God as a part of that person's life. God is not there just to tell a person what to do, but to give the way and the power for it to be done. See yourself that way and look at the possibility of a child in that way.

Who Puts It Together?

Each of the different views about the beginnings of life

(and there are others) are accepted by some people and rejected by others. Some have come to their conclusions after serious consideration and other after only casual thought.

No matter what view you accept, some will agree and other disagree with you. You'll have to be willing to live by your decision and yet live with others who have reached different conclusions. As the war is waged for and against abortion in picket lines, news headlines, and bumper stickers, you must not constantly be driven back to an old problem. Yet you cannot erase your experience. It will be a part of you; a part which, I believe, can be helpful to others as you share the spiritual and emotional values you gained from examining the value of life.

CHAPTER 8
Let's Pretend

The game "Let's Pretend" could be helpful to you now as you make your decision regarding the future of your pregnancy. Or the game could be dangerous. It all depends on which version of "Let's Pretend" you are used to playing.

"Let's Pretend" as a Cop-Out

Pretending that the problem doesn't exist is one of the many ways people have developed to avoid facing difficult situations. The strange thing is, in some cases, it works. But pretending the problem away only works if the problem wasn't real to begin with. Those who use their imaginations to create problems can also use their imaginations to get rid of them. Emotionally they have faced a big crisis and solved it, but actually nothing has happened.

Is there a possibility that you are not pregnant? Some have gone through great emotional distress regarding a decision about abortion only to find that abortion was impossible because it was unnecessary. If there is a possibility that you are not pregnant, find out for sure.

If you are pregnant, the problem can't be solved by "Let's Pretend." Don't try to rewrite history by thinking about how your life would be now had you never met that man, had not had sexual intercourse, or had been more careful about using birth control. Often the human mind wants to blank out certain experiences because they are too painful to face. In one way the ability to ignore a problem for a while may be helpful. It gives you a way to get used to the undesirable reality of your situation gradually. When you can't accept all the implications of a problem at once, the mind dams them up and let's them come through one at a time so you can handle each aspect and place it in its proper perspective.

Even as you face the reality of your situation you will occasionally need a rest from the burden of worry. Feel free to put things aside for a few hours, to enjoy an evening at a movie or a concert of your favorite music. But be honest with yourself. Don't use alcohol or drugs to help you "forget" for a while. When you remember again, you will have all the same problems with the possibility of a few more. If the pressures are too much for you to endure, find ways to relieve the tension that will help you rather than cause more difficulties. Maybe you can find help by talking to someone—not just about abortion but about politics, hobbies, or vacation. Maybe you can find an emotional rest by seeing a sad movie and crying over someone else's problems.Or see a funny movie so you don't forget how to laugh.

Don't pretend that a solution will "just happen." If you are serious about getting an abortion, a miscarriage would save you a moral decision. You may find yourself living in a pretend world that says you will have a miscarriage and all will be well. After all, other people have had miscarriages. Why not you?

You might even find yourself encouraging a miscarriage—by going horseback riding or lifting heavy objects or doing other activities you have heard might "accidentally" cause a pregnancy to terminate itself. But that game of "Let's Pretend" has two dangers. First, you might hurt yourself. Your body is built to protect the fetus from normal bumps and strains. Severe strain or physical force could harm you. Second, there is also psychological and emotional danger involved in an effort to trigger miscarriage. Doing so attempts to achieve the purposes of an abortion without facing the issues of an abortion. Later you might have second thoughts and wish you had the child. Then you blame yourself for causing the miscarriage.

(By the way, the miscarriage might happen anyway. If

you miscarry while you are thinking about an abortion, even without your encouraging a miscarriage, don't consider your thoughts responsible for the termination of the pregnancy. Miscarriages do happen, perhaps many more than most of us are aware of. A person who miscarries before having the opportunity to adjust to the idea of being pregnant can sometimes have guilt feelings—as though she had willed it to happen. Most miscarriages are the result of some incorrect development in the fetus. Often it is nature's way of preventing a problem birth.)

But pretending that a miscarriage will happen does not solve the concerns you now have. If a counselor's only goal were to prevent an abortion, pretending that the problem might be solved by a miscarriage could delay action long enough to make an abortion impossible. But I hope the goal is higher than that. You may have a baby because you want to, not because you are trapped into it.

Nor can you pretend away other problems. The birth of a baby will not solve problems in a marriage or another love relationship. Problems with parents, finances, and the like can be solved, but you can't pretend them away.

"Let's Pretend" as Decision Making

There is another way to play "Let's Pretend" that could be helpful to you now. You face a number of possible options. It is difficult to select only one of them. As long as you have not made a final choice you can pick the best part of each decision and live with it comfortably. But the fact is that each choice has disadvantages as well as advantages, and eventually you must choose one of the possible solutions by accepting both its good and bad results.

You can try each decision on to see how it fits your life by playing a controlled game of "Let's Pretend." The rules are: Select a possible course of action and pretend (for an assigned length of time, if possible at least a day, but maybe for only a few hours) that you are going to do it. Then live with your decision. Find out how you accept the consequences. If possible, talk to a friend or counselor who knows you have not made up your mind permanently but are using "Let's Pretend" as a way to evaluate your options. The person you talk to is not to persuade you to change your mind but to help you realize all the implications of the choice you are considering.

Use the same method to try out the other alternatives. In each case live as though you were totally committed to that course of action. Imagine how you would explain your decision to others. Find out if you would be relieved to have accepted that option. Or does the choice only increase your anxiety level?

As a guide for your "Let's Pretend" we will go through the options available to you. I will suggest possible good and bad results from each choice, but you will have to make the specific applications to your own situation. If I overlook one of your special concerns, you put it in. Some of the questions I ask may be sharp, but they are not intended to hurt you. Look at my questions as being like a doctor's gently squeezing a sprained arm until the patient yells. He doesn't do that to hurt the patient but to find out where the pain is so he can know where the help is needed. If some questions make you yell, be aware that it is an area in your life that needs special help. Don't hide from that question by resenting it. Get someone to help you work out the sore spot.

If You Got an Abortion

Let's pretend you decide to get an abortion. Say it to yourself: "I am going to have an abortion." Now try it in the past tense (that's the way you'll live with it): "I had an abortion."

Does the image you see of yourself as one who had an abortion fit the image you previously had of yourself? Does saying that you have had an abortion conflict with your views on the beginning of life and the value of life? Is there something special about your situation that you feel allowed you to get an abortion? Do you feel critical of others who got abortions? Of those who didn't get abortions under similar circumstances?

Will you always remember the date your baby would have been born? Some women think of that date often. Some with sorrow and regret. Others with gratitude that an abortion was available and a baby is not involved in their problems. Others are totally unaware of a date in connection with a past abortion. The question is: How will you react? Will you look at other children and think, "My child would have been that age"? Rather than freeing you from a child will an abortion tie you to all children?

Pretend you never have other children. Will an abortion give you regrets? Pretend you become pregnant again under similar circumstances. Would abortion be your answer again?

Also imagine what your decision will do to your relationships with others. Remember this is a controlled game of "Let's Pretend." Don't pretend everything will turn out the way you want. Don't imagine it will all be bad either. Only pretend the part about the decision. Look at the rest as realistically as possible.

If you have the abortion, what will it do to the relationship between you and the man of your life. If he is your husband, will he resent it? Will it be a block in your relationship? If it is a man you love, will the abortion change your view of him and his view of you?

Imagine the effect of your abortion on others. If you had an abortion, would you tell family and friends? If they found out from other sources, would it make an difference? Can you accept an abortion only if it remains a secret? Imagine what your relationship with God would be after an abortion. Will you want to avoid Him? Will you feel a need to make up for something you have done wrong? Will you feel He has helped you through a problem?

If the Baby Is Adopted

Now let's pretend another situation. You give birth to the

baby. Then the baby is placed in a home by an adoption agency. How would you be able to live with that decision?

Would you be able to stick to the decision? One reason some women want abortions early in the pregnancy is that they have not yet identified with the child. But as the pregnancy continues, the child becomes more and more real and demands more attention—even before birth. If a woman decides early in the pregnancy to give the child up for adoption, she may have second thoughts before the baby is actually born. Would you?

Would you be confident that the child was placed in a good home with parents who would give it proper care, education, spiritual training? Would you find yourself looking at children the age of yours and wondering if one of them is your child? Would you be able to "give" the baby up psychologically and emotionally as well as physically? Would the face that a husband and wife, though unknown to you, would be filled with joy when they received your child into their family, help you endure the feeling of loss? If you did accidentally discover where the baby was (an unlikely event), would you be compelled to identify yourself to the child as the "real" mother? Or would you accept the fact that an adopted child's real parents are those who share their lives with him or her?

Would you be willing to have the baby only if the pregnancy and the birth remained a secret? How would you react if the secret were revealed to your parents or others?

If You Keep the Child

Finally, let's pretend what would happen if you keep the child. Since this is "Let's Pretend" forget for the moment all the reasons why you have considered an abortion. Assume that you have the baby. Then face those issues that caused you to consider terminating the pregnancy. How would you live with them if you had no choice? Would they be as impossible or as difficult as you thought? Since abortion is an available option today, do you think that some take it as the fastest way out of a problem when another solution might have been better in the long run?

Of course, your answer depends on what your reasons for considering an abortion were. If you are married, both you and your husband should do the "Let's Pretend" together.

If you are not married, imagine yourself raising a child without a father in residence—at least for a while. Would you feel that it is too difficult to raise a child alone? Widows and divorcees do it. And some have problems. But then children in homes with both a mother and father have problems too. It is not the fact that a child is raised by a single parent or by two parents that makes the total difference. It is how the parent does the job in either case.

Would you feel shame about being an "unwed mother"? How would you explain your decision to the child later? Could you tell the child about its father in a way that would not degrade the man in the child's eyes? Would you lie about the father to make him greater than he was?

What about finances? Who can and will help you? Will you lose a job while you are giving birth? How will you hold down a job and provide care for a small baby?

Also, if you have the child because you feel that abortion is morally wrong, will you feel that God owes you some special favor because you have obeyed His law? God does have many special favors for you—but not because you have earned them. Don't fall into the thought-pattern, "I did what was right, now God has to hold up His end of the bargain." When you do what is right, because it is right for you it is your own reward.

If you raised the child, would it be living evidence of your own mistake and would you therefore blame the child? Would you feel you had to give up many parts of your own life to have the baby and rear it; therefore, that child had a special obligation to you? Recognize that such an attitude could make life difficult for the child. A study of children born after the mothers were denied abortions has shown that most of the children have troubled childhoods and few became happy adults. The reason for the children's problem was not that an abortion was denied. It was that the mothers did not or could not overcome their own problems (the ones that made them request the abortion), and therefore they were passed on to the children. If you are to make a sacrifice for the child, you must give a willing sacrifice not just an investment for your own future. To give up something important for yourself and then resent the child that required your self-denial is a "sacrifice out."

As you pretend what would happen if you kept your child, remember that most problems have solutions. Often the solutions are difficult, but then most worthwhile things are difficult. You have to decide if you can work for a solution and if you are willing to. Will the problems that make you consider an abortion now become problems for the child later if you don't get an abortion? Or are they problems you will have whether or not you get an abortion? Will the responsibilities of a child add to the pressures of your own situation? Will those pressures be so much that you will destroy the child's life later? Being a parent under any circumstance requires sacrifice and devotion—and a lot of hard work. Are you willing to be the kind of parent who is willing to give for the sake of the children? But are you also one who would give willingly and not as a martyr? Will the emotional strength you need now not to "give up" your baby leave such a permanent mark on you that 20 years from now you will still feel, "I can't give up my baby"?

Pretending that you keep the baby is the most difficult because it plunges you into the unknown. The other solutions have terminal dates. When the abortion or adoption is completed, all you have to do is learn to live with the memory. But keeping the child has long-range results. It offers the chance for greater sorrows or greater joys.

How Long Can You Pretend?

"Let's Pretend" must be a short game. It is a device to help you reach a decision, not escape from the problem of making up your mind. As you live with each of the possible courses of action for a short time, evaluate. Which does the most to solve the problems that trouble you most? Use the "Let's Pretend" method to project into your future to consider your needs then. Find out which decisions solve some problems by creating others for later. Then your pretending has helped you face reality.

CHAPTER 9
And Now to Decide

One of the big messages of this book, in case you haven't noticed, is: "Don't rush into a decision!" The time factor is an extra problem for a person considering an abortion. If you are going to terminate the pregnancy, it must be done as soon as possible. However, if urgency becomes an overriding issue and your only concern is to grab an option, the real issue of an abortion will be lost.

Ask Questions Now

To follow the advice, "Get the abortion now and ask questions later," may offer an easy way out now. But when you do ask the questions later, you may give answers that make you wish you had chosen a different option. Take the time now to ask questions and find the best answers possible. And remember, some questions have more than one answer.

However, the time must also come for you to make the decision. The fact that you're near the end of the book doesn't mean the time is right now. Perhaps important parts of your situation have not been included here. If not, I hope the more general circumstances covered have helped you examine your own set of facts. You can write them into the record. It could well be that some subjects mentioned in this book created more problems for you than they solved. If so, seek additional help. Find someone to whom you can explain your special need.

Not to Decide Is to Decide

If you find yourself continually delaying a decision

because you need to talk to more people and read more books, be aware. You may be deliberately putting off making up your mind. Evaluate your past habits of decision making on less important issues. Do you often have a difficult time reaching a decision? Do you try to get other people to make choices for you? Do you jump at the first or the easiest solution that comes along? Do you decide on one course of action one day, change it the next, and change the change the following day? All of us have our own odd ways of making up our minds. Most are not necessarily harmful unless they become so extreme that they prevent us from reaching good conclusions—*good* meaning a decision that solves more problems than it causes. Look at your track record of making choices so you can understand the extra conflicts you may be putting on yourself now.

And also remember, "Not to decide is to decide." The most immediate choice before you is to have an abortion. If you select another option you have more time and also the possibility that even other choices will become available. Without an abortion some of the problems that trouble you now may be solved before the normal end of your pregnancy. Or you might be in a better situation to live with the problem later on.

On the other hand, in a limited amount of time (find out from a doctor when that time expires) the option of an abortion will no longer be available to you. If you cannot decide to have an abortion, yet cannot make the statement, "I will not get an abortion," you are caught on center regarding a choice that will soon pass you by. Perhaps not to decide is the easiest way to avoid an abortion if you recognize deep down inside that you don't want one. But delay your decision with an honest awareness that not to decide is to decide. Don't play games with yourself by delaying a decision until after an abortion is no longer possible, then regret that you didn't terminate the pregnancy. Your future decisions cannot be built on the shaky foundation of a decision that you pretend you didn't make.

Your Conscience Also Needs a Guide

No matter how strong your reasons are for wanting an abortion, you must balance them against your views about the life developing in you. Remember the subject of chapter 8: Is the fetus human or prehuman? If you accept the life in you as a baby, then abortion would be murder in your own mind. Such a view does not necessarily mean that you would not be able to get an abortion. We often do things that are against our moral judgment because other forces (real or imaginary) override our consciences. If you violate your conscience, you will cause problems for yourself later.

Also give special consideration to whether or not an abortion will solve or prevent all the problems you are facing. Abortions have often, even before more liberal laws were passed, been approved to protect the physical health of the woman. The mental health of the woman has also often been used as a legal reason for termination of pregnancy. However, in many cases the abortion has not solved the psychological problems that the woman felt were reasons for her abortion. And in an alarming number of cases the abortion added to the emotional wear and tear.

If You Have an Abortion

If you decide to have an abortion, there will be further decisions. When? Where? Who? Even with legal abortions available the back-alley abortion clinics are still in business. Many of them may be operated by people with good intentions. They may have even helped some women when no one else would. But the fact remains that they do not have the proper training, equipment, and/or cleanliness. Every two out of three are not good enough.

Some still choose to have abortions the dangerous way because of guilt feelings. Others because they want a secrecy they fear is not available through legal channels. I have tried not to demand or plead in this book. But I would do either if it would discourage you from a medically unsafe abortion. If you are determined to have an abortion, go to a doctor who is well regarded in your community. He will give you proper medical advice.

Also, if you decide to have an abortion, be aware that you will need continued counsel after the event. If you have established a relationship with a counselor or friend who understands the situation, ask that person to share your feelings after the pregnancy is terminated. You will need someone to listen to the details. For some reason we all have to tell others the details of our surgeries. This one may not be as easy to discuss at coffee break, but it will have to be talked about. So look for a listener.

You should also allow for the possibility that your views may change later. The experience of an abortion may make you grateful that it was available or it may make you regret either the need for an abortion or the decision to have done it. Do not let yourself get in a position of always having to defend your course of action. Be willing to grow from it, knowing that growth always involves change. You have not been right 100 percent of the time in past decisions. Your security as a person does not depend on your being totally right this time.

If You Keep the Child

Now consider the possibility that you decide to keep the child. If it is too late for an abortion or if you feel that you cannot willfully end your pregnancy, the next option is for you to become a mother. The decision not to have an abortion still leaves open the possibility of adoption. But we'll consider that later.

Can you decide not only to give birth to and keep this child, but also to be glad you have the child? Being a mother has its problems even in the best of circumstances. It also has its joys. The advantages and disadvantages of parenthood must be considered together for a realistic picture. You must face the extra expense of a child, but also know that having money by yourself is not so much fun. Children take a lot of extra time, but when you are alone time has little value.

Examine other problems that you are considering and see if you can find matching joys.

The special questions for you to face are: Will the problem that has made me consider an abortion become a problem for the child? Or will it remain a problem for me and therefore cause problems for the child? Would a baby add extra strain on me and make my problems greater?

The "Two Pregnancies" Theory

To help answer those questions, consider the "two pregnancies" theory about the development of human life. The theory gives you an opportunity to also consider the possibility of two abortions.

First an example: A female kangaroo gives birth to a baby when it is not fully developed. The newly born baby leaves its mother's womb but remains in her pouch. The time the baby kangaroo spends in the pouch is like a second pregnancy. The mother continues to protect and nourish the baby until it can permanently leave her.

A human baby is born after a nine-month pregnancy. It leaves its mother's womb and enters the pouch of the family for a second pregnancy. The family continues to protect and nourish the developing child during the second pregnancy that lasts 16 to 20 years. For a person to become a mature adult he or she must go through the period of development in both pregnancies. A decision not to abort the first pregnancy should be connected with a decision not to abort the second. The concern for the life of the fetus must be followed by a concern for the life of the child.

The fact that an abortion is available to you may make you face issues many women in your situation ignored a few years ago. You are not forced to have the baby. If you decide to give birth to the child and be its mother, you are doing it because you want to. As you have considered the problems connected with this pregnancy, think about the blessings that could come from it too. Certainly, you'll probably have an occasional doubt that you did the right thing. But don't let the child feel the burden of those doubts. Remember, you have made a commitment to keep the child and you must also be willing to make additional commitments as they become necessary.

You must also be willing to allow the child to complete the second pregnancy and leave the pouch. If your own life looks messed up right now with the cold reality of missed opportunities replacing dreams of achievements, you may want to keep the baby as a substitute batter for you in the game of life. But you cannot raise a child to do what you were unable to do or to be what you were unable to be. Though the child receives life through your body, it becomes his or her life. You have the joy of seeing it get started.

If the Child Is Adopted

There is a compromise option between abortion and keeping the child. If you cannot have an abortion and you cannot keep the child, you can give the child to another family for adoption. The baby may complete the first pregnancy in your womb and the second in the pouch of another family.

At one time adopting was the accepted solution to an unwanted pregnancy. The unwed mother gave her baby up for adoption. The physically, mentally, or financially ill married woman sent the child to "Grandma" or "Aunt" to live. Abortions were seldom available then. The stigma of a child born out of marriage reflected against both the mother and the child.

But today adoption is last in the popularity poles of those who face an unwanted pregnancy. Relatives are not as available, or not in the situation, to take an extra child. There is not as much social criticism of a child born to an unmarried woman. The ratio of families who want to adopt to children available for adoption varies according to location. But in all places the number of parents who want to adopt far exceeds the number of children available.

A Waiting Family

Have you seriously considered completing your pregnancy and then letting another family have the child? Let's look at your situation from that point of view.

Since you are deeply concerned about your own problems right now, it might be difficult for you to think about the family that is at this moment waiting for a phone call from an adoption agency. Yet it might help you face your own problem if you thought about their concerns for a while. One out of eight married couples are unable to have children. Many of them want a baby. They do not want you to suffer. They are sorry that you have this difficulty in your life now. They do not want their happiness to be built on your sorrow.

Instead the couple that is praying to receive a child through adoption would like to see themselves as helping you even as they see you as helping them. They want you to have a way of knowing that your baby can live and be well cared for. They want to help you avoid facing the decision and the fact of abortion or of rearing a child in difficult if not impossible circumstances. Though you will never meet them and they will never meet you, they will think of you often. They will thank God for your willingness to give them your child.

What Will the Child Think?

I may sound cruel to you even to think the words, "I will give away my baby." Most of the women I know who have chosen abortion rather than allowing their child to be born for adoption have done so because they could not give the child away. One woman said, "No mother could give away her child." I have listened to their views and I respect their opinions. No one who has not been in the position should be so bold as to claim the only right answer. Especially when it is *his* answer. But I do ask you to consider the relative emotional stress of abortion and of giving the child for adoption.

Part of the problem is that the longer you are pregnant the more real the child will become to you. An abortion stops your emotional involvement early. But if you carry the baby full term and give it away, you may feel its unseen eyes accusing you of forsaking it. You may think that the child will blame you. Or that the child will assume you were a prostitute or an unlovable and unloving person.

An abortion would prevent the child from ever accusing you. If the child does not exist, you do not have to wonder what he or she is doing. Yet remember that nonexistence can be thought of in two ways. First, nonexistence is that which never existed. One of those couples that cannot have children may refer to the children they hoped for but never had. They never had a child except in their dreams.

Second, nonexistence means that which no longer exists. If an abortion stops an existence (as discussed in chapter 7), nonexistence has a different meaning. We have no easy answers to the questions about the beginnings of life. There are contradictions in our views about miscarriages, abortions, and stillbirths. Christians believe that death is not the end of life. Once life has started, it is eternal by God's grace in Christ. You must know whether you regard an abortion as a way to prevent a child from ever existing on earth or as a way to stop a child's present existence on earth.

You may feel that a baby would prefer not to live in this world than to know that it had been given away by its mother. But remember, you are thinking abour life during a troubled time in your own existence. Right now you may not be too happy that you were born. We've all felt that way at one time or another. But we survive the problem and find new joy in living.

If you place your baby for adoption, you are not abandoning it. You are seeing that it receives excellent care. Of course, not all adoptive homes are perfect—others aren't either. But the child will have a home and family. When the child grows up and is aware that the mother who gave him birth also gave him away, he will also be aware of the fact that his mother could have had an abortion. But that child's life will always be evidence that you had enough love to give life willingly.

You may have second thoughts about this decision too. Some mothers have later tried to trace down a child they have given for adoption. But if you make the decision with a conviction that it is best for you and the child, then you can live with it and be glad about the option you chose.

Of course there are other problems in giving birth to the child for adoption. You need a place to stay until the baby is born. You need medical attention and maybe financial help. There are people available to help you with such problems. Your doctor, pastor, or other counselor can help you and can refer you to additional help.

The Decisions That Follow

The big decision you make regarding your present situation will be followed by many more decisions. Maybe each of the smaller decisions will not seem as important, but in the long run they also will have a great impact on your life.

It is important for you now to make the best possible choice as you consider your own situation. But it is also important that your decision fit into the plan you see in your own life. Let this decision lead you toward your goals in life, not away from them.

PART II

CHAPTER 10

Counseling Those
Who Are Considering an Abortion

Some counselors are specialists. They work with people who have a specific problem, such as alcoholism, marriage problems, unwanted pregnancies. Counselors who specialize already know they can deal with the problems that come with their speciality. And they can get the training to help people with that problem.

Other counselors are general practitioners. Clergy, teachers, those who work for community agencies, those in private but not limited practice find themselves facing a broad range of counseling subjects. In one day they may talk with people facing a variety of problems. And since one problem seldom exists alone, they often counsel a person with a wide range of interrelated difficulties.

Abortion and Counseling in General

The general practitioner in counseling today will have to face the issue of abortion. Some will come for counsel after they have had the abortion. Others who are considering an abortion will want to talk about it first. A few will come in behalf of family and friends.

Two easy ways to have a good batting average in abortion counseling are available.

First, put a sign (either literally or figuratively) outside your office: "Abortion is still murder." That will solve the abortion problem for the counselor. If a clergyman, he can say, "We don't have the problem of abortion in our

105

congregation." And he will probably be right. Those who have the problem will either leave the parish or keep their problem a secret. Meanwhile, the pastor can feel sure that he has not contributed to the death of unborn babies.

The other way to solve the abortion problem is to have a sign, again either literally or figuratively, outside your office: "Abortions approved here." Those who have had an abortion often need to be told that they did the right thing. Those considering an abortion often go from counselor to counselor until one agrees that an abortion is necessary. All the better if the counselor can say that God said it was okay too.

The counselor who follows the "all abortions approved" philosophy can point to a large number of people who come for help. Such counselors can show that they helped many women be free both from unwanted children and guilt.

But the counselor who is not concerned about his or her own batting average but is concerned about people (both unborn babies and the woman who is pregnant but does not want a child) is better off without a sign. Unless the sign says, "I hear and I care."

The Need to Refer

Each counselor in a general practice should decide whether the subject of abortion can be included in that practice. No person can be expected to cope with every situation. There are valid reasons why some should not counsel with those considering an abortion. Maybe your own personal or family experience with the subject gives you a slanted or prejudiced view. If you have been personally involved, you may understand others in the same situation better. Or you may still have to defend your own decision or involvement. If each counseling case rekindles an old problem for you, you should not be involved.

Other experiences could interfere with abortion counseling. If you want to adopt a child but none are available because "everyone gets abortions these days," you may not be objective. If you feel you would not exist if abortions had been available before your birth, you may be on shaky ground.

If you cannot deal with the subject of abortion, you should have a place to refer those who need counseling on the subject. As in any referral, make it clear you are not rejecting the person. Instead you are showing that you want the person to receive a better source of help.

On the subject of referrals: When you do counsel with those considering an abortion as parts of a broader professional role, you should know specialists in abortion-related fields, i. e., legal, medical, spiritual. Then you can either refer the counselee to others for answers to special questions or obtain the necessary information to share with the counselee.

The Role of the General Practitioner

While the general practitioner in counseling should use the resources of the specialists, the one in the general practice also has some unique opportunities unavailable to the specialist.

In the first place the nonspecialists often have titles other than counselor—a term that seems to be problem centered. The titles pastor, teacher, doctor (as in family doctor) indicate other relationships that are not crisis related. As a counselor working in a broader field you will be contacted by many who would not go to a specialist. Even those who eventually go to a specialist for counseling often start the process with a counselor they already knew and trusted.

Preventive Counseling

In the second place the nonspecialist can deal with the subject, in this case abortion, in a much greater arena. Perhaps the most important counseling a pastor, teacher, and many social workers do regarding abortion is in the general area of education on related subjects. They have numerous opportunities to do preventive counseling in less emotional situations than those where a decision must be or has been made. Those who must face the abortion decision are better off if they have a background of information learned before they were personally involved.

Most people who have abortions today have had no previous encounter with the subject to help them in the decision. Abortion has been a hidden and forbidden subject. Schools and churches felt no need to teach why abortion was wrong, because everyone (including those who gave and received abortions) agreed they were wrong.

Now the situation has changed. Abortions are legally available. Many church, political, and educational leaders believe that abortions should be available to anyone who wants one. Those who would never have considered an illegal abortion suddenly ask, "Why not?"

Few adults or teenagers today have read an article, studied a lesson, heard a sermon, or even been in a serious discussion about the beginning of human life. The articles, lessons, sermons, and discussions available show we don't have a pat answer. But people should be acquainted with the questions and know the reasons for the different answers. The most important education regarding abortion does not even approach the subject of abortion itself. First, people need to sharpen their own understanding of life. Families, churches, and communities must foster an attitude of respect for human life.

Other areas where education is needed to lay the groundwork for an understanding of abortion include family life and conception control. (The term "conception control" is used here rather than the more common "birth control" because in one sense abortion is a form of birth control. Here we are speaking of preventing conceptions, not preventing births.) Even in our open society today where sex can and is discussed anywhere, young people receive little preparation for the total sexual relationship in marriage and family. The most important and lasting relationships on earth are those in the family; yet few young people receive training in family living other than the example of their parents. Time spent in family education is effective preventive counseling on abortion.

Years ago most people would have assumed that inexpensive, effective, and available means of conception control would have eliminated all abortions. Yet as the availability of methods to control conception has increased, so also have the number of abortions. Obviously, more education is needed in the use of conception control methods. Time spent teaching in this area is also effective preventive counseling on abortion.

Those involved in shaping the moral code of the community need also to be aware of the influence of violence on people today. Most adults have grown up on a diet of radio, TV, and newspaper reports of bombings and body counts from the battle zones. War and its violent deaths have been a part of our education. Many have been trained to cheer the glories of war.

We have seen the abuses of capital punishment. We have seen deaths in racial and economic struggles. Our entertainment in movies and on television regularly show violent death as a part of the American scene.

Is it any wonder that our consciences have been deadened to the subject of killing? Abortion is calmly accepted by many because it fits in the pattern we know. Those who want to speak out on the value of human life in the area of abortion must show the same concern for life in other areas. Emphasizing the value of human life in all situations as a part of the moral fiber of our community is a necessary part of preventive counseling in the area of abortion.

From another point of view our acceptance of violence has increased the need for abortions. Those who honestly see the horror of child abuse find it difficult to wish birth on a baby who might be born into such a life. Many children are abandoned, mistreated, ignored. Those who oppose abortion should also be willing to face the reality of child abuse.

Looking for workable solutions to the problems of children who are abused by their parents is also an important way to give preventive counseling regarding abortion. Our society needs to speak for the rights of children. Education is needed for parents who cannot cope with their responsibilities. We must make it easier for parents who cannot be good parents to give their children to others who can.

These problems reflect some of the major difficulties in our society. You as a counselor cannot solve them. But as you work in the crisis situation of those facing abortion, you can also be aware of your opportunities to provide guiding principles to others to keep them from becoming involved in the same problem. As you work with the symptom by helping an individual face the issues involved in abortion, you can also work to fight the sickness in the society as a whole.

Direct Counseling

But as you help an individual, you are also providing another person who will be a help to the total society. In your concern about the big issues of abortion as it affects everyone, you must not lose sight of how terminating or not terminating a pregnancy affects the life of an individual. Your primary role as a counselor relates you to the individuals who are considering an abortion. You can see your responsibility in three ways:

First, to prevent the abortion—and save the life of a baby.

Second, to make the abortion as easy and painless as possible—and help the woman.

Third, to help the woman reach a decision according to her values and the set of circumstances she is in at the time.

Either of the first two options would probably be easier for both you and the counselee, and certainly take less time. However, the woman or family making the decision will also have to live with the decision. You can continue to help her/them live with the decision only as long as you are not blamed for it. She needs to make the decision herself, knowing you will not reject her in case she does not decide the way you think she should.

110

Even if abortion is against your moral principles, you need not reject her. Never can you accept people (even your own children) on the condition that they agree with you on all moral issues. Establishing this fact before the decision is made is important because the woman should not feel forced into guessing what you want her to do. Help her find what she wants to do.

During your counseling session you must be able to share something with the counselee and she must be able to share something with you. As counselor you are to be directive enough to make progress during your conversations together but you must be open enough to let the woman make the agenda.

Between the two of you abortion must be discussed from two points of view. One approach must not dominate the other. The counseling sessions should be directed to bringing the two views into focus so they form one, clear image.

The first position, which is to be presented by the counselor, covers the objective facts about abortion. The counselor should know, or be willing to find, all the general information needed. This includes legal matters, such as adoption, support of a child by the father, and the legal conditions of abortion in their state. In some places consent of parents are required for minors seeking abortions, and of the father if he is known.

The counselor also needs to be aware of medical facts and resources. Where can an abortion be obtained? What is the cost? What are the circumstances? What method will be used? When must it be done?

The counselor must also give moral and spiritual guidance. Theological statements need to be applied in practical language so the counselee can understand why some people object to abortion and others approve. She should realize that some will criticize her for having an abortion, others will criticize her for having the baby. The counselor must help the woman understand her own moral principles. Does she think that abortion is moral, or is she willing to consider going against her own conscience? Is she choosing the lesser of two evils? If so, are there other choices?

Though the counselor's job is to be a resource of objective information, he or she need not share all the information available. Don't impress the counselee with your warehouse of facts. Wait until she shows what information she needs, and provide it. Save the rest for the next person.

The counselor must also help the person considering an abortion present her views. She has less experience in counseling situations. Don't be so eager to share what you know that you do not listen to what she knows.

The counselee's view of the situation is the personal, subjective one. While you have applied the view of abortions in general, she is considering one specific possibility—her own. You must listen to and understand her feelings, her situation, and her concerns. Even if it is a typical, textbook situation for you, it is her own personal problem. She needs to be able to spell out the details. And you need to listen. Don't assume she fits into an established category. She needs to know not only that you are aware of what she is thinking, but also that you understand why she thinks as she does.

The two views, the objective and the subjective, of abortion must be considered together until the situation of each is applied to the other. The facts and the feelings must be harmonized to the extent that neither is radically violated in the final decision. You must understand how her individual situation fits into the entire moral, legal, medical question of abortion. She must see how the thinking of many others has an influence on her situation.

When the two views come into focus, she will make the decision.

CHAPTER 11
Theological Statements

Many people turn to theologians for a final answer to the abortion question. All major protestant denominations have issued statements on the subject that show a general area of agreement. Most want to caution against abortion, but at the same time they recognize that under specific situations abortions are necessary. While individuals or groups within most churches can be readily identified as either strongly proabortion or equally strong against abortion, few church bodies have adopted extreme positions.

Following are three examples of a theological approach to abortion by Lutherans. An attempt to include statements from major churches met with the frustration of limited space in this resource book. Also such position papers are subject to constant revision. For the latest official stance of any church body, write to the denomination's national headquarters. If you represent a denomination, your church's official statement on abortion should be added to this book.

From: **A CHRISTIAN VIEW OF ABORTION**

For the Christian there are definite theological implications in any consideration of abortion. He needs to give consideration to the Biblical doctrines of creation, the origin of life, God's providence, God's relation to evil, death, the dignity and worth of the individual, and the destiny of man. Thus our attitude toward abortion is affected by a wide variety of Biblical teachings.

113

Creation

The Biblical doctrine of creation has a bearing, for it tells us that the matter making up the embryo and fetus was created by God. Matter is not eternal; it had a beginning; it came into existence by God's almighty power, Genesis 1:1

Moreover, it was by God's almighty power that the matter which He created became alive, Genesis 1:20-25, 27. The Bible is very clear, too, in pointing out that human life is on a higher level than plant and animal life. Both plant and animal life were created when God spoke, Genesis 1:20, 24. But when it came to the creation of human life God's action was of a special kind which the Bible describes as forming man from the dust of the ground and breathing into his nostrils the breath of life, Genesis 2:7.

Not only is it clear from Scripture that matter came into existence by God's almighty power and that it acquired the qualities which we call life by God's almighty power, but Scripture also tells us that new life originates by God's creative power. When He said "Be fruitful and multiply," Genesis 1:28, He not only gave a command but also the power that life might continue. Conception is in the hands of God. Man may indeed prevent it and be a secondary cause in effecting it, but he is not the primary agent in bringing it about, Psalm 127:3. The giving of new life is God's prerogative.

Thus what Scripture says of the origin of life and of the way in which it continues must be given serious consideration in any discussion of abortion.

Providence

The doctrine of providence is also involved. It is God who governs the universe. The earth's future is finally determined not by what happens in Washington or Peking or Moscow, but ultimately its future is determined by the almighty God who sits in the heavens. God not only governs the universe, but His providence extends also to the affairs of individuals. It is He who permits conception to occur, and His

114

will is thereby directed both to the conceptus and to the parents. God has not abdicated; He is not the watchmaker God, who has set the world in operation by creating it and by establishing the scientific laws by which it is ordinarily governed and has then withdrawn. He is very much a part of the operation of these laws. That is what the Bible teaches when it discusses God's providence.

In functioning, God of course employs secondary causes or means by which He preserves and directs the things that He had made; thus we speak of divine concurrence. Scripture is very clear in describing the relation of God to the secondary means which He employs. For while in the divine act of concurrence both God works and the means work, the operation of the means is not coordinated with that of God but rather subordinated so that the secondary causes work only so far and so long as God works through them, Psalm 127:1. Thus conception occurs as a consequence of coitus, but only because God permits the egg and the sperm to unite. Moreover it is God who determines the genetic content of the particular egg which is fertilized and of the particular sperm which effects fertilization. The operation of the laws of nature which make conception possible are not detached from the divine will but are simply God's will exerted in the being and action of His creatures in order that they may be preserved both in their existence and operation. That conception occurs, that the individual receives the particular set of genes from his mother and from his father, that certain conditions exist during his prenatal existence in the womb are a part of God's providence, not the result of chance. (Psalm 115:3 and Psalm 135:6)

God and Evil

We must recognize that as a result of the Fall evil can and does occur. We cannot say that God is responsible for sin when He allows man to commit sin. We cannot blame God when a child is conceived outside of marriage. We cannot blame God for defective genes which, while they are not the result of a particular sin, are the result of original sin and the consequent departure from the perfection which God created. We cannot blame God for disease which may handicap the fetus or for damage that may be done by drugs which his mother ingests. God concurs in producing the effect but not the defeat. The former is clear from Acts 17:25-28, the latter from such sections of Scripture as Deuteronomy 32:4 and Psalm 92:15. Thus God's concurrence in permitting a conception and in permitting the development of a fetus under circumstances which appear to be evil—the development of a defective child or the burden of a pregnancy on a mother whose health will be adversely affected—is essentially a refraining from acting on God's part, inasmuch as He does not place insuperable difficulties in its way and prevent it from occurring.

At creation all life was in harmony and at peace with all other life; there was no conflict of values in which a child might be pitted against his mother. Since the Fall, though, life may be pitted against life; the order of creation has been altered. Sickness and suffering are not the will of God but rather the reverse of the real will of God, even though God still carries out His will. If the bearing of a child actually poses a real threat to the life of the mother, we cannot say that her death is the will of God. If illness were indeed His will, then all medical action would be rebellion against God.[1]

Man's Role

It is true that God works through men, and it is in this connection that human judgments must be reached and decisions made. We may very properly seek to ameliorate the evil which comes with God's permission. We may relieve pain through analgesics. We may seek to prevent the spread of disease and attempt to cure it when it occurs. Man is not passive in creation, but he is God's steward and caretaker. He is to subdue the earth and to have dominion over the fish of the sea and over the birds of the air and over every living thing that moves upon earth, Genesis 1:28. He was placed in the garden to till it and keep it, Genesis 2:15. Because man is the foremost of the visible creatures, he has a special obligation over against creation. He is God's caretaker and steward and is expected to be active rather than passive. He may not sit back with hands folded and plead that evil comes from God; he must take active steps to ameliorate the evil that he sees about him.

But his actions must always be taken in the light of the Biblical framework. Before he determines to terminate a life through abortion he must recognize that life is a gift of God and that children are gifts of God to their parents. The life which he is considering taking is God's gift to the conceptus, embryo, or fetus. The parents must recognize that this child is God's gift to them, Psalm 127:3. God's gifts are good; it is man's corrupt mind that judges some of them to be evil.

But what about the defective child? Is God being good to him in giving him life? The Bible gives us no reason to deny that God's gift of life also to this individual is good. God tries no one above his ability to overcome the trial, 1 Corinthians 10:13. The cross that the individual must bear is often the fire that brings out and purifies the gold of faith. It shows the individual how really helpless he is and how dependent he is on God for everything he receives.

This is also true of parents who may feel that another child or a defective child is a burden impossible for them to bear. The resources which the Christian has in his God are boundless; God can and does turn apparent evil to good, Romans 8:28. While God does not send the evil it comes with His permission because He knows that He will be able to bring good out of it, Genesis 50:20.

Death

Also to be considered is what Scripture teaches about death. Not only is the beginning of life in God's hands but also its end, Psalm 31:15. Man has no right to terminate a life unless he is acting as the agent of the state in its God-given rights and responsibilities or in self-defense or in the defense of his loved ones. Even the individual may not take his life or consent to the taking of it. While the Bible does permit the taking of life, it clearly points out that this may not be done arbitrarily and without very good reason.

The Dignity and Worth of the Individual

Still another theological consideration is the dignity and worth of the individual for whom Christ died. God knows us as individuals; He has written our names on the palms of His hands, Isaiah 49:16. He cares for us even before birth, Job 10:10-12. Scripture tells us that God so loved the world that He gave His only begotten Son to die for it, John 3:16. Each individual has dignity and worth; each has been the object of God's love, not only in creating him but also in sending His Son to suffer and die for him. The conceptus, the embryo, the fetus also have a God-given dignity as well as a God-given right to live. Bonhoeffer says: "Destruction of the embryo in the mother's womb is a violation of the right to live which God has bestowed upon this nascent life."[2]

This dignity is what Thielicke calls an "alien dignity," not an "intrinsic" dignity. It is not something which belongs to man but rather something which has been given him by God, Deuteronomy 7:7f. To the Christian this makes it an even more important dignity, one which he is very hesitant to deny or infringe on.[3]

The Sanctity of Life

A very important consideration in this connection is the sanctity of life. Both plant and animal life are gifts of God, Genesis 1; human life is a special gift and is especially sacred, for God not only spoke when He brought it into existence, but He formed man from the dust of the ground, made him in His image, and breathed into his nostrils the breath of life, Genesis 1:27; 2:7. God regards the violent termination of a human life as a very serious matter. He cursed and banished the first murderer, Genesis 4:11 f., and He threatens with

118

death all those who violently take the life He has given, Genesis 9:6.

Abortion brings us face to face not with the question of whether life dare be prevented at its beginning but rather whether human life dare be destroyed. "The decisive point is the sanctity of life itself, including germinating life."[4] Artificial abortion is "the most serious assault on the order of creation."[5] No human body may ever be regarded as a thing, an object that might fall under the unrestricted power of another human being and be dealt with solely as he sees fit.[6]

Baptism

God's concern is shown in His institution of the Sacrament of Baptism. Faith is indeed worked through the Word, but it is not possible to communicate with an infant through the Word. In this situation Baptism serves as the special means of grace by which the Holy Spirit may be active and create faith in the heart of this child with whom we cannot communicate in the usual oral manner through the Word. God wills that that child come to eternal life, and so He has established a special means of bringing the Gospel to him. It is true, of course, that God can and does work outside Baptism. We have every confidence that when God decides to take the life of a child before birth through a miscarriage He will in response to the prayers of those parents work faith in that child even though he may not be baptized. We know that the Holy Spirit can work in the heart of an unborn child, Luke 1:41, and we have every confidence that the prayers for spiritual blessing on that unborn child, which Christian parents speak as soon as they know conception has occurred, will be answered (James 5:16; Luke 11:13; 1 John 5:14). Yet the Sacrament of Baptism is another indication we have of God's concern for and interest in infants who also are destined for eternal life.

Parental Privilege and Responsibility

Once impregnation of the ovum has taken place the

question is not that of possible parenthood; man and woman *have* become parents. They must think not only of the life of the fetus but also of their status and responsibility as parents. An office and duties have been thrust upon them. The question is not "whether a proffered gift of parenthood can be ... accepted but rather whether an already bestowed gift can be spurned."[7] Marriage itself involves an acknowledgment of the right of the life that is to come into being—a right that is not subject to the whims of the married couple. Bonhoeffer points out that unless this right is acknowledged, marriage ceases to be marriage and becomes a mere liaison.[8] The sin does not begin with the abortion itself but with the refusal to say "Yes" to a gift God has bestowed and to a responsibility imposed by Him.

Justification by Faith and the Promise of Forgiveness

Can the sin of abortion be forgiven? Of course it can; only the sin of deliberate and persistent unbelief bars from eternal life, and that only because it refuses the proffered grace and forgiveness. But this is certainly no license to sin, Rom. 6:15f., and no license to take the matter of abortion lightly. We must seek guidance from God's Word, we must wrestle with Him in prayer over our decision, we must examine repeatedly our motives, and we must be willing to follow His commands and our conscience. The real blessing of grace is not that it is a license to sin but rather the assurance of forgiveness if we have sinned inadvertently. An abortion may indeed bring feelings of guilt even when we are convinced it is proper and necessary; letting a mother die or suffer a severe handicap may also bring feelings of guilt. For these guilts there is the assurance of forgiveness.

There are other considerations as well. There is our inability to evaluate objectively our motives. To what extent is love for one's self playing a part? Is the mother really concerned for the welfare of her small children when she considers terminating a pregnancy which seriously threatens her health? Or is she thinking only of herself? Is her husband thinking of the children? Or is he moved by the bother of another child or by his need for the love and companionship of his wife whose life and health are threatened?

We all have difficulty in making our wills conform to God's will. Our response to His commands all too often bears the marks of our hardness of heart. (Matthew 19:8)

If we sin because we have difficulty in an objective evaluation of our motives or because of the hardness of the converted heart, God offers His forgiveness. We continue to be preserved by God's patience, 1 Peter 3:20, to the end that He may have mercy. (Romans 11:32; 2 Peter 3:9; Ezekiel 18:23)

All these theological principles need consideration when the question of abortion is discussed and especially when we are faced with a practical situation. There is always danger that broad principles will be overlooked under the pressures of a particular seemingly urgent situation. When we consider that life has been created by God, when we remember that God has taken special pains in creating human life, when we recall God's role in governing the universe and in ruling the affairs of individuals, and when we believe that all things work together for good to them that love God, we will terminate the life of a conceptus, embryo, or fetus only under the most unusual circumstances. True, there are times when a life may be terminated without violating the Fifth Commandment, but we must be sure that our action does not ignore the broad theological principles which we deduce from Scripture.

John W. Klotz, Chapter 4, "Theological Implications," Contemporary Theology Series (Concordia Publishing House: St. Louis, 1973), pp. 34-40. Used by permission.

From: **THE PROBLEM OF ABORTION**

How then does the Christian go about making decisions in the area of abortion? As in all Christian action he works between two poles—his motivation in Christ and his concern for human needs. He moves between his faith and the facts in the human situation. Through faith he has been given genuine love for his neighbor, a servant-style of life that is dedicated to the alleviation of human suffering and need. At the other pole he finds his neighbor set within the contemporary scene with its welter of facts and forces.

Viewing the situation, the pregnant woman (with her mate) seeks to respond positively to such demands upon her as these: love, procreation, and the new life within her; her other children and her home; the laws and mores of the community; her own physical and psychological health; her doctor's advice. Viewing the same situation, the medical man adds such factors as these: the statistics, the array of medical resources, the case histories, his own experience and competence, his own convictions about fetal life. In and through all these complex factors the Christian—pregnant woman or doctor—seeks to respond to God. Knowing that God is at work within his immediate environment and within all the circumstances of life, the Christian tries to find evidences of God's workings that will be clues for his own decisions. He seeks to respond in his decision to what God is doing by fitting his own action into God's actions. Since sinful human wills have also entered into the making of any situation, the Christian needs to combine his best knowledge and most mature wisdom with persistent prayer and conscientious struggle with the issues, if he hopes to discern God's hand in the matter and to receive the guidance of the Holy Spirit in reaching a decision. Should a certain pregnancy end because the father has died? Should the particular heart condition of this woman mean the end of her pregnancy? How does one give moral weight to statistical probabilities concerning malformations of the fetus? Does the population explosion represent God's will that there be more human lives or is it his warning to men to limit procreation? Does the population explosion have any relation to the question of a particular abortion? Do a woman's fears and guilt feelings sometimes determine whether abortion is called for? It is in struggling with questions like these, as they impinge upon any given situation, that one assesses the facts and looks for God's will for one's decision.

Fortunately, the Christian does have certain resources to guide him in decision-making, though his actual choices remain his own free and creative responses to God in a specific situation. For one thing, he has the perspectives of Christian theology—an understanding of God's dealing with men and the world, which comes from God's revelation in Jesus Christ. Such perspectives include the message of Scripture and all the theological interpretations and patterns of conduct worked out by Christians throughout two thousand years of church history. In this accumulated Christian wisdom lie new vistas of insight, broader and deeper avenues of understanding, to bring to bear upon any present experience. Here are resources to be taken seriously, though they do not in themselves determine a Christian's course of action.

The second set of resources consists of the communities to which a Christian belongs, channels within which his decision must take place. To them he owes a loyalty which requires that he, on the one hand, take their standards and recommendations seriously, and, on the other hand, act responsibly in the shaping of the community's patterns of thought and action. Besides the home that is directly affected by a pregnancy, two other communities help shape the decisional life of the Christian woman considering abortion, as well as her doctor and all who enter into the decision. One of these is the contemporary Christian community. Members of the church at any time and place should function like a team with a common perspective and a common purpose (the loving service of human needs for Christ's sake). The basic approach to any ethical problem should root in the corporate life of Christian worship and study, in discussion together, and in a common style of action on many fronts of daily life. Such experiences should prove helpful even in the unique circumstances of a particular question of abortion.

The second is the civic community, represented in the

laws of state and nation. The Christian seeks to be law-abiding, since he realizes that civil law represents God's law, however imperfectly, and serves God's purposes of social order and an approximation of justice. He will uphold good laws and work for the establishment of laws that serve the welfare of his fellow citizens and of all humanity. This means that he will obey the abortion laws under which he lives unless clear duty under God calls for disobeying them. It also means working to make the aborion laws the best ones possible in a particular society.

Medical men have a particular responsibility in the shaping of proper and wise abortion laws, and indeed of all laws that affect human health and life-and-death. For the doctor belongs to the medical profession—the third significant community. To it he is responsible and from it he draws resources. Doctors move together in determining standards of competence, habits of practice, ethical patterns and their influence upon the body politic. The doctor who is a Christian has a special responsibility under God to shape and respond to this powerful medical community of which he is a part. Indeed it may well be that the doctor can find the strongest, most intimate resources for specific decision-making in his discussion and teamwork with fellow American Christian doctors—those who share the same three significant communities.

Ultimately, however, he makes his own decisions within the limitations of his situation. Informed by a conscience that has been nurtured in the Christian community, responsibly related to the medical profession as a whole, the Christian doctor decides for himself before God. He has the right and obligation to withhold his skill and to refuse to operate when he believes it would not be to the best interests of the patient, the fetus, and society itself. But when his consideration of all the factors brings him, by whatever agony of decision, to believe that it would be best to operate, then he should proceed in Christian freedom. The issues will not usually appear in blacks and whites but in shades of gray. Frequently he will have to choose the lesser of two evils. The ambiguities will sometimes persist to the end. But when he forms his decision responsibly, he can move ahead with a clear conscience, knowing that God in his mercy will remove all guilt and forgive him the evil that was unavoidable in the situation. This may mean allowing a pregnancy to continue only to have it take the mother's life, or conversely, killing the fetus in a futile attempt to save a woman's life. Or it may mean advising a woman to bear her child even though the chances of a normal birth are quite problematic. If he has acted upon his honest convictions, he has done his duty and need not experience guilt. He has answered God's call and made his personal Christian decision.

Nonetheless, it is of grave importance that there be broad agreement about public policy in such a crucial matter as abortion. Here the resources mentioned—theological perspectives and the communities of Christians and doctors—should prove particularly helpful in developing broad guidelines for the next decades of American society.

Sometimes these are called "middle axioms" or "working principles," but "strategies" is a better word because it more easily suggests flexibility and change. Such strategies vis-a-vis issues of abortion will relate to the public and the law, to medical attitudes and practice, and to Christian decision-making about abortion.

As one focuses the light of the already outlined theological perspectives upon the previously described situation, certain strategies appear wise for Christians, medical people, and the citizenry as a whole.

On the one hand, a "biologism" that severely limits all practice of abortion is unacceptable as theologically invalid and sociologically unrealistic. There is no good theological basis for assuming that every conception unambiguously represents God's will. And when this position influences public policy it widens the dangerous gap between official policy and actual practice.

On the other hand, the practice of providing abortion at

the will of any pregnant woman is also unacceptable, because it does not take seriously enough potential human life and does not protect incipient human life from the whims and fears of its mother. Conception and the new life which results are neither unimportant in the eyes of God nor without social consequences that involve the public interest.

The strategy which commends itself is a move from the second position toward the third one, from the present practice of stretching the meaning of therapeutic abortion toward the advocacy and practice of a carefully defined and socially protected "compassionate" abortion. As has been pointed out, this third position takes seriously the rights of fetal life but gives priority consideration to the needs and circumstances of the pregnant woman, including her present family responsibilities. It could provide a theologically, ethically, and sociologically sound stance for the Christian to take in the shaping of public policy and medical practice, as well as in his own decisions concerning abortion.

Frederick K. Wentz and Robert H. Witmer, Chapter 4, "Ethical Stance and Strategy," Board of Social Ministry/Lutheran Church in America (New York, 1967), pp. 17-21. Used by permission.

From "ABORTION: THEOLOGICAL, LEGAL, AND MEDICAL ASPECTS"

Ethical decisions call for the most competent application of both the ability to make judgments and the willingness to be guided by the principles derived from the revelation of God's will. To that end men have been endowed with reason. They are expected to use this gift for purposes of making choices on given issues. In making up their minds, however, they must be guided by more than human calculations. In the matter of abortion this means that such alleged dangers as overpopulation and dire predictions of an impending shortage of food are not decisive, since such estimates and projections may suffer from the fallibility inherent in any human enterprise.

This is not to suggest that ethical guidance offered by the church sets out to ignore or to denigrate competent judgments made by professional persons on the specific issues under consideration. What it does indicate is that God is still the Lord of history and that He can and often has upset human calculations. In the process of ethical decision-making, therefore, persons will be well advised to give greater weight to basic principles set forth in Scripture than to conclusions reached only at the hand of man's reckoning.

Living as Christians calls for trust and obedience toward that God who, through Word and Sacrament, offers man salvation in His Son, Jesus Christ, and who reveals His will for man in Holy Scripture. Holy Scripture does not present us with a detailed set of regulations for abortion and many other complex ethical problems. It does, however, offer principles of enduring validity and authority. Responsible ethical living therefore calls for making personal choices on the basis of validly established principles rather than following a detailed set of regulations in a servile way. Accordingly, these guidelines are intended to set forth those principles of God's revelation that should guide individuals in making decisions and judgments on the question of abortion as a theological, legal, and medical problem.

Report of the Commission on Theology and Church Relations, The Lutheran Church—Missouri Synod (St. Louis, 1970), p. 5. Used by permission.

CHAPTER 12
Points of View

It is an oversimplification to divide all of those involved in the abortion debate into two camps—either proabortion or prolife. Many who have arrived at the same conclusion came to their position via different routes. To understand the issues regarding abortion, the reasons one is for or against the possibility are as important as the conclusion.

This chapter shares a wide variety of reasons that have been given to defend either proabortion or prolife conclusions. The excerpts included here are to show the wide range of questions that must be considered to present the total picture of the abortion issue. A word of caution: A person considering an abortion must establish the agenda for counseling sessions. Do not show your wide experience by introducing every idea presented in this chapter.

Caution #2: Out of fairness to the people quoted here remember that the quotes come from longer works. The quote used was chosen to present an idea, not to give the author's total view.

From: ISSUES IN THE ABORTION DEBATE
Opponents of liberalization

1. Life begins at the moment of conception; the fetus has a right to life; abortion is murder ("lynching in the womb").
2. It is just one step from abortion to euthanasia; legal abortion reflects and encourages declining morality and loss of reverence for the sanctity of life.
3. Promiscuity will be encouraged by legal abortion; sexual

misbehavior should be punished ("she had her fun, now let her pay").

4. In this bottle (slide) you see a fetus, a human fetus. This one is 4 (6, 8, 10, etc.) weeks old. It already has a heartbeat (fingernails, capacity to experience pain, etc.) just like you and me.

Proponents of liberalization

1. Life began eons ago; the question is when does a human person begin—some say at conception, some at nidation, some at quickening, some at viability, some at birth, some at a later date; the assignment of personhood is arbitrary and differs among faiths; if abortion were considered by society to be murder, 30 million American women would be behind bars—the total accumulated number of women who have had abortions during their reproductive years. If fertilized ova were considered persons, we would require registration and burial of all spontaneously aborted fetuses (including many expelled with late menstrual flow). A hydatidiform mole starts as a fertilized egg, ends as a mass of cells, and could in no way be described as a person. A blueprint is not a house, an acorn is not an oak. DNA is not a person.

2. Abortion and euthanasia are separate issues (though determining the end of the human person is as difficult a question as determining the start); we set speed limits at 60 MPH and do not necessarily then move them to 70 MPH (one step does not necessarily lead to another); reverence for life includes concern for the quality of children born and consideration for the rights and wellbeing of women unwillingly pregnant.

3. Fear of pregnancy is notoriously inefficient as a deterrent to sexual behavior. Why should the woman be punished and not the man? Why should an innocent child also be punished? Does the punishment fit the crime?

4. There are three parts to this argument: (1) it is upsetting to see a fetus in a bottle; (2) it is emotionally threatening to see

129

the similarity between a fetus and ourselves; and (3) the weeks at which certain stages of development are reached is presumed to be "news" and of scientific, educational importance to the audience. (1) Those not trained in medicine would be equally upset to see an eyeball or a segment of intestine in a bottle, or projected on a screen; we should not confuse disgust with moral objection to the procedure of abortion; most would not want to see an appendectomy performed, but that does not mean we oppose all surgery. (2) We should not be surprised to find a human fetus looks like us; rather we would be amazed if it resembled an elephant. But a dead body also looks very much like us, yet that does not prevent us from cutting that body, as in an autopsy, since the *person* is *no longer* there— as the *person* is *not yet* there in the case of a fetus. (3) Back to the central issue of personhood and rights; other non-persons (pigs, cows) have toenails, heartbeats, and the capacity to feel pain (some say a fetus can feel only pressure, not pain, but we're not sure), yet these factors alone do not prevent the destruction of such entities.

Proponents of liberalization

5. In a pluralistic society one religious faith should not be permitted to impose its views on others by law, though it may make every effort to do so by persuasion.

Opponents of liberalization

5. This may be true for less serious issues on which the various religions differ, but on the question of abortion, those who believe it to be equivalent to murder are duty-bound to make every effort, including legislative restriction, to prevent its occurrence.

Opponents

1. Legal abortion abroad has not eliminated illegal abortions.
2. If abortion had then been legal, Beethoven wouldn't have

been born, and possibly some of you senators here wouldn't have been born, and my lovely third child wouldn't now exist.

3. Abortion is genocide; it is an attempt by people in power to eliminate poor and Third World people.

Proponents

1. Mere modification doesn't, in fact, eliminate illegal abortion; it only makes a dent. But far-reaching liberalization (as in Japan and Hungary) does drastically curtail it (as reflected in decreased deaths and hospital admissions for "incompletes"), but the residual can be attributed to remaining restrictions and lack of privacy within the legal registration system.

2. And possibly Hitler wouldn't have been born either. We do not miss the many persons not born because they were spontaneously aborted. If Beethoven's father had coughed at the critical moment, a being other than Ludwig would have been born instead.

3. Under restrictive laws, poor women suffer most, as reflected in their disproportionate mortality and underrepresentation in the few hospital abortions performed under restrictive laws. Legal abortion will be made available on a voluntary basis to those women who want to use it—there is no suggestion for coercive measures in a call for liberalization.

Proponents

1. Legal abortion will decrease the number of unwanted children, battered children, child abuse cases, and possibly subsequent delinquency, drug addiction, and a host of social ills believed to be associated with neglectful parenthood.

2. Legal abortion will decrease the number of illegitimate births.

3. Legal abortion could decrease the tragedy of the birth of deformed children.

4. Legal abortion provides the only humane disposition of a pregnancy resulting from rape or incest.
5. Under restrictive laws, rich women with know-how obtain safe legal or quasi-legal abortions, while poor women bear unwanted children or are butchered by back-street abortionists.
6. A bad law, unenforced and unenforceable, fosters disrespect for the law in general.

Opponents

1. Society would do better to make substitute provision for unwanted children with adequate institutions and benefits to enable each child to have a warm and loving home. Many women who do not want a child when they discover their pregnancy do change their minds and love the child when it is born—and vice versa. It cannot statistically be proven that children born to women denied legal abortion fare any worse than those presumably willingly conceived; irresponsible parenthood stems from many causes and should be dealt with accordingly; unwanted children can turn out to be creative geniuses, contributing much to society.
2. Although we are alarmed by the surging increase in illegitimacy, society must find alternate ways of preventing it—sex education, adequate contraception—or of dealing with it once it occurs—adoption services, child care allowance, jobs for unwed women.
4. Deformed children have as much right to live as others; many deformed persons lead normal and constructive lives. If you sanction the disposal of deformed fetuses, you may soon also decide to do away with the elderly and the useless, or the non-productive adult.
4. Tragic as these cases may be, that is not adequate justification for the destruction of human life. (Opponents do, however, sometimes find rape so abhorrent that they would make an exception.)
5. That is a matter of discriminatory application of the law,

132

not of its substance. Neither group should seek or obtain an abortion, safe or unsafe, legal or illegal.

6. Many laws are difficult to enforce; that is not sufficient justification for their eradication.

Proponents

7. The population explosion compels us to take every means necessary to curb our growth rate. Since contraception alone seems insufficient to reduce fertility to the point of no-growth, and since population experts tell us that eliminating unwanted fertility would go a long way toward achieving replacement fertility, we should permit all voluntary means of birth control (including abortion) so as to avert the necessity for coercive measures.

8. Legal abortion will result in a reduction in welfare rolls. (As has often been remarked, the abortion reform effort makes strange bedfellows.)

Opponents

7. The United States is not experiencing a population explosion. Problems of pollution and environment degradation are due more to other causes (increased affluence) than to population growth. Growth is good for business. If growth seems detrimental to our quality of life, then we should step up family planning programs utilizing contraception only, avoiding the necessity for including abortion. If you can use abortion to control the size of the population, then you will also justify euthanasia and genocide.

8. There you are—genocide, the elimination of "un-desirables." Society must make adequate provision for its needy—not merely ensure their non-birth.

Rights and Responsibilities
Opponents

1. The father should have some say, or equal say, since it's his fetus too.

133

1. He's not a "father" (any more than she's a "mother") until a child is born. He may contribute 50% of the genes, but he does not have to bear and care for the outcome. A husband's consent clause violates the woman's right to control her own body. Some husbands may not be present, some partners may not be husbands, and in case of disagreement and a husband's denial of abortion the woman is subject to compulsory pregnancy and involuntary servitude.

Proponents

1. A physician has the right to practice medicine as he sees fit; he should not be limited in his choice of advice and precedure if a medical solution to the problem presented to him is feasible. He or she also has the responsibility to refer a patient for care if he or she cannot in good conscience perform an abortion. Public funds should not be used for facilities where no abortions may be performed.
2. The family has a right to determine its own size, using all technology available.
3. It is a woman's right to control her body, to determine the timing and extent of her own fertility.

Opponents

1. As noted earlier, the availability of the means does not justify their use; one need not apply a medical solution to a social, economic, or personal problem. At the very least, we demand a conscience clause in any liberalized law which would prohibit discrimination against nonparticipating hospital personnel; this is not adequately insured by the Medical Practices Act or the Hosptial Code.
2. No such right exists; it is the moral duty of each married couple to engage in responsible sexual relations, which need not necessarily result in uncontrolled fertility.
3. The rights of the individual woman must be weighed

against other rights—those of the fetus and of society to uphold its moral integrity.

Complied and edited by The Population Resource Center of Planned Parenthood of Minnesota (St. Paul), 1973, pp. 30-32. Reprinted from "The Major Issues and the Argumentation in the Abortion Debate," appendix to "Abortion and Public Policy," Emily C. Moore, *New York Law Forum*, Vol. 18, No. 2, 1971. Reprinted by permission as modified by Population Resource Center.

From: "ABORTION . . . A PERSONAL DECISION"

Since life is a continuum, to argue as to "when life begins" during human development is to pursue an exercise in futility. However, since the entire case against abortion revolves on this issue, I will discuss it briefly. No one will dispute the *potential* of a fetus (or an egg or sperm for that matter). An aborted fetus might have become a Beethoven *or* a Hitler. Like Hardin, I consider an embryo or fetus comparable to a set of blueprints up to the stage of independent viability. In its phylogenetic development the embryo traces stages in the evolution of man; it is certainly, with its gill slits and other primordial appendages, something less than a complete human being for a considerable period of its development. We are not dealing with a *black* or *white* moral issue but with *shades of gray*. The fetus becomes less primordial and more human with every week of gestation. At what point in development is it so human that it should be granted legal protection? The answer to this question varies from person to person, dependent primarily on one's personal philosophy and religion. Discussion of fetal development rarely, if ever, changes anyone's personal view as to when meaningful life begins.

The panegyrics of those who oppose abortion, regardless of circumstance or stage of gestation, are essentially a discourse on the rights of the fetus ("baby"). One must respect their right, in their personal lives, to view the fetus as equal to the woman; however, equal respect should be given those who consider the life, welfare, and desires of the pregnant woman of considerably greater moment.

Robert Benjamin, M.D., "The Rights of the Fetus," *The Bulletin of the St. Louis Park Medical Center,* Vol. XVII, No. 2 (St. Louis, 1973). Used by permission.

From: "ABORTION IN THEOLOGICAL CONTEXT"

Six or seven years ago I knew little about abortion since it was only beginning to become a major issue in America. We were occupied with two other major social issues—racism and war. In a bit more than a decade Americans were attempting to eradicate racism which had been a festering, cancerous sore eating away at the moral fiber of their country for centuries. And, at the same time they became committed to a war posture in Viet Nam which brought internal conflict and confrontation at home of a sort hardly known before in our history. We were not threatened so much by defeat as by internal destruction.

On both issues it came out that I was on the right side—I was against the war and against racism. In both cases I was an activist—not militantly, but involved . . . .

And when abortion became an issue, there was a strong tendency for those who had been antiwar and antiracism to be proabortion. It was the "liberal" and socially concerned thing to do.

At this point I fell out of line and I departed from my "liberal" friends, for the very same substance of the Christian faith which had informed my decisions on race and war had now begun to shape my thinking on abortion and consistency demanded that I not favor abortion personally, and that I not foster it publicly through a position which left the matter of the killing of another human being a private, individual decision.

Having been involved with blacks who had been DEHUMANIZED by word-games, i. e., defined out of existence by being made property instead of persons, I could not start that same game with the unborn child. I could not remove it from the human sphere of concern, nor from the Christian sphere of "neighbor" by calling it a "piece of tissue" or a "glob of protoplasm. . . ."

The abortion controvery looms as an issue larger than abortion itself. It has become the focal point for the questions of life and death which face us in the entire area of biomedical ethics. It is a sign of what appears on the horizon as a moral struggle of cosmic proportions reaching into every corner of the world. There is a clash between the "old" and a "new" morality. And it apperas to me that here we can discern the shape of a struggle between Christian faith and secular humanism. . . .

C. J. Eichhorst, ForLIFE, Inc. (Minneapolis, 1974). Used by permission.

From: **A LETTER**

I take sharp issue with bland assertions made by many theologians, . . . that every pregnancy is the will of God. Many unwanted pregnancies are the result of behavior contrary to the will and law of God. There are natural laws of the creator which, for example, produce ovulation at about midcycle in most healthy women. Coitus, even under the most abnormal situations, at this optimum time of the cycle may, without proper prevention, result in pregnancy. This is not the will of or design of God when people act contrary to his laws of human behavior, but neither does he act to prevent pregnancy from occurring.

Elfred Lampe, M.D., November 21, 1973. Used by permission

From: **"THE PROBLEM OF ABORTION AFTER THE SUPREME COURT DECISION"**

Many efforts have been made to determine just when, in this process, distinctively human life begins. The Supreme Court, as we have seen, confessed its bafflement over this question. In fact, much depends upon how one wishes to define the term "human," and this in turn often reflects the ethical position that one is inclined to take. The fertilized egg can be said to be already human in the sense that it is the product of human intercourse and has the potential and the programming to develop into a human being (and not any other kind of being). Looking at a later point in the process of development, it is certainly significant that by the eighth week, the fetus not only has all its internal organs as well as a recognizably human external form, but also shows electrical activity in the brain, and will respond to stimuli; on these grounds, it could well be considered "human." In another sense, however, even the new-born infant is not yet *fully* human, in that it is not yet able to utilize the precious gift of speech, nor does it know the rich context of conscious interpersonal relationships that we associate with a fully human life. If one argues that abortion poses no ethical problem because the embryo or fetus is not yet fully human, this argument, from the standpoint of strict logic, could be used also to justify infanticide. If one does not wish to accept this conclusion, then—as the theologian Paul Ramsey has emphasized—one should re-examine the underlying premise.

We live in a "throw-away society," which is used to treating many things cheaply because they can easily be replaced. The Christians will be on guard against adopting any such attitude toward the child-that-is-to-be within the mother's womb. Rather, their attitude will be one of respect, and even reverence, for nascent life. Properly understood, all of our modern scientific knowledge of the developmental process should only serve to reenforce that fundamental sense of awe and gratitude that the ancient Psalmist had—on the basis of far less information—when he wrote: "I will praise thee, for I am fearfully and wonderfully made" (Psalm 139:14). . . .

Finally, the church's word will be one of acceptance and support for its members who make conscientious decisions on this issue, regardless of the side on which their decisions fall.

For the church is called to be a community of reconciliation, also for those who disagree about the problem of abortion.

Franklin E. Sherman, Division for Mission in North America. Lutheran Church in America (New York, 1974), pp. 14-15, 24. Used by permission.

From: TESTIMONY . . .

It is my conviction that a constitutional amendment will help to safeguard the concerns of our constituency for innocent, defenseless life which has an intrinsic value and dignity beyond being "wanted." To use wantedness in connection with human beings is to reduce them to objects. We usually want *things:* a new coat, a car, a hamburger. To want or not want people is to dehumanize them. Further, to use wantedness in connection with human beings is to tell us nothing of that human being. I might describe you as weary, or biased, or gentle. However, the minute I say you are unwanted I am no longer describing *you,* but I am telling you something about *myself.* Unwantedness measures *our* attitudes and feelings. The fact that the Supreme Court allows for the elimination of a whole segment of the human family tells us nothing about those children, but rather tells us what kind of people we have become.

I know that we can't pass a law that would make all children wanted. But I am reminded of an incident in 1964 when a United States Senator said, "You can't pass a law that will make me love Negroes." Negroes replied, "We don't care whether you love us or not; we need a law that will keep you from being able to kill us and will protect us from all kinds of discrimination." I am concerned as a mother; I fear for the children of our country for whom also the law is teacher. Are they not learning that sanctity of life may be enjoyed only by those who are planned? That reverence for life extends only to those who are perfect? That quality of life takes precedence over life itself?

Jean Garton, Testimony Before the U.S. Senate Subcommittee on Constitutional Amendments, March 7, 1974. Used by permission.

ABORTION OR THE UNWANTED CHILD: A CHOICE FOR A HUMANISTIC SOCIETY

The anti-abortion movement believes that the fetus, even in its embryonic stage of development is human life and that any deliberate termination of embryonic or fetal life constitutes an "unjustified" termination of human life—that is, homicide. Conversely, proponents of abortion deny that the fetus is human life, particularly during its embryonic stage of development, and therfore believe that the termination of fetal life does not constitute homicide. Further, proponents of abortion justify the termination of fetal life by asserting that the woman has the ultimate right to control her own body; that no individual or group of individuals has any right to force a woman to carry a pregnancy that she does not want; that parents have the moral responsiblity and constitutional obligation to bring into this world only children who are wanted, loved, and provided for, so that they can realize their human potential; and that children have certain basic human and constitutional rights, which include the right to have loving, caring parents, sound health, protection from harm, and a social and physical environment that permits healthy human development and the assurance of "life, liberty, and the pursuit of happiness."

These conflicts of "rights"—namely, the presumed rights of the fetus, the rights of the woman, the rights of the child, the presumed rights of adults to unlimited reproduction, and the rights of society—need careful consideration in evaluating the morality of abortion. How do we order the priorities of competing "rights"? Since rights confer obligations, does the failure to meet those obligations mitigate or abrogate the rights that gave rise to those obligations?

For example, when conception occurs in a uterine environment known to be adverse or a child is permitted to be born into an adverse environment, both of which threaten or deny the child's basic human and constitutional rights and opportunities for normal human development, should moral and constitutional questions be raised concerning the rights of such parentage? Is the right to parentage absolute? Do adults who are incapable of responsible behavior (for example, the severely mentally retarded) have the right to bring into this world children who will be neglected and abused and who will become infant- and child-mortality statistics? Is it not more moral and humane to prevent a life than to permit a life that may experience deprivation, suffering, and perhaps a brutal early death, which many of our child-abuse and infant- and child-mortality statistics reflect? Is mere physical existence our highest goal and greatest moral burden? Or is the quality of human life our highest goal and greatest moral burden? What are the social and moral criteria for justifying the sacrifice of human life? Perhaps the justifications for a "just war" should be considered in relation to certain arguments for and against abortion.

These questions of moral behavior, like that of abortion itself, are unlikely to be resolved by religious convictions or theological doctrine, since such convictions and doctrine vary considerably among free people and are, at best, arbitrary in their formulation and implementation. The extensive debates on abortion clearly indicate that no philosophical, religious, or scientific consensus exists concerning the question of whether fetal life is human life. A similar lack of consensus exists concerning the moral and ethical nature of the abortive act. Further, the US Constitution does not permit the legislation of religious beliefs or doctrine.

Consequently, it would appear constructive to examine the abortion question from a different perspective. Specifically, what are the effects of denied abortions—that is, of compulsory childbirth or of being an unwanted child—upon the development of the child; what are the consequences to society when parents are denied the right to have only wanted children; and what are the characteristics of societies that permit abortion in contrast to those that punish abortion. An examination of these questions from the perspective of the behavioral and social sciences, rather than from that of theology, should provide a basis to evaluate the merits of abortion on different grounds and to clarify the motivations and some of the social and psychological characteristics of the proabortion and antiabortion personality.

<h3 align="center">Consequences of Denied Abortion:
The Scandinavian Study</h3>

One of the most important studies that tried to evaluate the consequences of being an unwanted child upon the development of the child was conducted in 1966 by H. Forssman and I. Thuwe of the Department of Psychiatry at Goteburg University in Sweden. Therapeutic abortion was officially legalized in Sweden in 1939 and liberalized in 1946 to include mental-health criteria. These Swedish investigators examined the development of children from birth to age twenty-one who were born during the years 1939 to 1941 to mothers who had applied for abortion but were denied. The sample included one hundred and twenty children, who were compared with a control group of children whose mothers had not applied for abortion. Of the unwanted children, 27 percent were born out of wedlock, whereas only 8 percent of the control children were born out of wedlock.

The statistically significant differences between the unwanted and the control children can be summarized as follows:

1. Sixty percent of the unwanted children had an insecure childhood, in contrast to only 28 percent of the control children. Criteria for an insecure childhood included official reports about unsatisfactory home conditions: the child was removed from the home by authorities; the child was placed in a foster or children's home; the parents were divorced or deceased before the child was fifteen; the child was born out of wedlock and never legitimized.

2. Twenty-eight percent of the unwanted children had

received some form of psychiatric care, compared to 15 percent of the control children.

3. Eighteen percent of the unwanted children were registered with child-welfare boards for delinquency, compared to 8 percent of the control children.

4. Fourteen percent of the unwanted children had some form of higher education, compared to 33 percent of the control children.

5. Fourteen percent of the unwanted children received some form of welfare between the ages of sixteen and twenty-one, in contrast to 2.5 percent of the control children.

6. And finally, while 68 percent of the control children showed none of the social disabilities mentioned above, only 48 percent of the unwanted children were free of such characteristics.

It is worth noting that many of the differences listed were found in different social classes. In summary, unwanted children are more than twice as likely to suffer the social, emotional, and educational disadvantages as wanted children, on a variety of measures. Unwanted children appear to present certain costs to society: increased delinquency, a higher number of welfare recipients, a more poorly educated citizenry, and a greater number of psychiatric problems.

Child Abuse and Neglect: Consequences of Being Unwanted

The killing of a child by its parents is an extreme outcome of being unwanted and is the final act of child abuse. Roman civil law recognized the right of the father to maim and kill his offspring (*patria potestas*), and a number of cultures have practiced the killing of female infants because they were valued less than male infants. Ceremonial sacrifices of infants and children have been documented in a number of cultures, and Abraham's willingness to kill his son for religious purposes is a biblical case in point. But the killing of one's own child in a modern civilization is uniformly met

143

with revulsion and horror—even though child abuse, which is the precursor of filicide (the killing of one's own children) and neonaticide (the killing of the newborn), is widespread today. The central issue here is the role of abortion in preventing unwanted children and helping reduce the incidence of child abuse and infanticide. It should be recognized that being "wanted" and being "unwanted" are difficult psychological concepts, and E. Pohlman's " 'Wanted' and 'Unwanted': Toward Less Ambiguous Definition" should be consulted for a more extensive treatment of this subject.

Phillip J. Resnick, in a study of one hundred thirty-one filicides, found that 49 percent were associated with "altruistic" motives—for example, to relieve suffering; 21 percent were attributed to parental psychoses; 26 percent were attributed to the child's being "unwanted," which includes the child-abuse syndrome, and 4 percent were attributed to revenge on the spouse. Statistics, however, fail to convey the horror and tragedy of parents killing their own children, particularly when it could be prevented.

Several of the case histories are so grueling that they cannot help but raise the question of whether it is more humane to prevent human life than to compel it into an existence that possibly could result in a cruel and painful death. Dr. Resnick cites several means by which infants and children are killed. He states: "Head trauma, strangulation, and drowning were the most frequent methods of filicide. Fathers tended to use more-active methods, such as striking, squeezing, or stabbing, whereas mothers often drowned, suffocated, or gassed their victims."

It is unnecessary to catalogue the atrocities that are sometimes inflicted upon unwanted children. In Dr. Resnick's study of thirty-seven neonaticides, he found that 83 *percent of infant killings were attributed to being "unwanted" by the mother;* 11 percent to psychoses; 3 percent to "accidental" murder (child abuse); and 3 percent to "altruism." These infanticides must be seriously considered in any discussion of abortion, since for some people they may seem to be the only alternative to compulsory pregnancies.

The 1965 national fertility study reported by L. Bumpass and C. F. Westoff showed that, for the years 1960 through 1965, 22 percent of all births were unwanted by at least one spouse. This rose to 48 percent and 55 percent for families with five or six children. The greater proportion of unwanted births was reported from low-income and poorly educated families. Such family characteristics are serious impediments to providing quality care for children . . . .

Given the alternative to abortion—that is, the birth of unwanted children, with all the adverse implications—it is clear that abortion is a beneficent and humanitarian act that values the *quality* of future human life more than the *quantity* of future human life. It is worth mentioning that the principle of the prevention of human life has its precedent in scripture—albeit in a different context—namely, Judas' betrayal of Jesus Christ: "It had been good for that man if he had not been born" (Matthew 26:24). Should this not be equally true for many children who are doomed to a life of misery and abuse, and for some who may meet an early violent death.

James W. Prescott. This article first appeared in *The Humanist*, March/April 1975 issue and is reprinted by permission.

From: "THE UNWANTED CHILD SYNDROME IS A MYTH"

Far too often in pro-abortion propaganda the unwanted child syndrome is linked to the battered or abused child syndrome. Even a cursory review of the literature concerning abused or battered children would indicate that in most cases children who are battered or abused have been wanted children; that the essence of the problem rests with the parent or someone else; certainly not the child.

Dr. Edward F. Lenoski, trauma consultant for the Pediatric Pavilion, Director of Children's Emergency Service at the Los Angeles County/USC Medical Center and assistant professor of pediatrics at USC School of Medicine discussed some of the characteristics of the Battered Child when he spoke to a meeting of CARES, the Los Angeles County/USC Medical Center Auxiliary. Some exerpts from his speech are given below:

> Which babies do you think are most often abused— planned or unplanned?

> There's the group which says, 'We're going to get the car paid for. We'll get all that French provincial furniture. We're going to get everything paid for, and then we're going to have a baby . . . and we'll have one of those frilly bassinets.' Then there's another group: 'I missed a period. Whoops, a mistake, another baby.' The unwanted pregnancy.

> Anyway, it turns out that 90% of the beaten children were planned pregnancies . . . because, you see, it's one short step to say, 'Look, you little fink, I saved and saved to buy this bedspread, and you just moved your bowels on it.' Whack. You see, it's easy to blame the baby.

> The Planned Parenthood [sic] is scared about this, because since the introduction of the Pill, child beating has gone up threefold.

John E. Harrington, *Marriage and Family Newsletter*, Vol. 3, Nos. 8-10 (Aug. 1972). Used by permission.

From: "ABORTION: A HELP OR HINDRANCE TO PUBLIC HEALTH?"

I do not believe there is any question when biological human life begins. It is at conception, by which I mean when a sperm fertilizes an ovum. To say that it begins at any other time is biological nonsense. Sperm alone do not lead to the birth of babies, nor do ova alone. It is when the two are fused that the process of human development starts and it ends at death. I will only add that with *in vitro* fertilization the truth of this statement is even clearer than it ever was before.

But I suspect that this undoubted fact is not what the abortion debate is about. That the fetus is alive and not dead is undoubted. If it were dead, an abortion would not need to be performed and there would be no child to raise. That the fetus is biologically human is also clear. It simply puts it in a category of life that is different than the cat, the rat, or the elephant. So the human fetus represents undoubted human life and genetically it is different than any other animal life.

But I think what those who do not oppose abortion mean to actually convey is that this life is not sufficiently valuable to be protected. It has no value, no dignity, no soul, no personhood, no claim to be protected under the Constitution.

That is not a *biological* question. That is a *value* issue. The issue is hidden under such language as "meaningful" life or "potential" for life, or "quality" of life. What is at stake goes far beyond the issue of abortion. The question is this: Are there to be *live* (not dead) *humans* (not rats, cats, etc.) who are to be considered devoid of "value," "dignity," "soul," "meaningfulness," "protection under the Constitution" or whatever phrase or word by which one wants to describe the inclusionary or exclusionary process?

This is fundamentally why I am opposed to abortion. It is because it attaches no value to live biological human entities. I am not among those who believe that all human life must be kept alive my machines at all costs, but I am opposed to a philosophy that proceeds to actively kill existing human life for utilitarian purposes. This cheapens all covenants existing among men.

Furthermore, I am puzzled by the selectivity with which some would apply abortion. If the fetus does not constitute truly human life, I do not see why so many would deny abortion on demand. It is sometimes said we do so because after the 13th week, or at some other arbitrary time, it becomes dangerous. But we do not prevent women from becoming trapeze artists for financial reasons, we don't prevent men from becoming football players or boxers for financial reasons. I frankly don't see why we should prevent

147

women from incurring mortality or morbidity risks in abortion if they thought it was financially advantageous to them. But the problem is, of course, the fetal killing.

I also don't understand why genetic counselors would approve of abortion of fetuses if they are abnormal, but 96% would not if the fetus is of the wrong sex. If a fetus of the wrong sex does not represent human life, why shouldn't one abort it? I don't understand those who say they don't like abortion and would only use it as a last resort. If abortion does not kill human life, why should it be a *last* resort and not a *first* resort? Some might feel better with one abortion per *year* than a pill per *day*. So I see this constant ambivalence about abortion, but I understand the ambivalence, because I think the vast majority of people now know how babies are produced and they can't quite avoid the issue of the fetus all of the time.

So the fundamental question is whether we shall assign no value to certain categories of human existence.

Andre E. Hellegers, M.D., testimony before the U. S. Senate Subcommittee on Constitutional Amendments, April 25, 1974. Available from the National Committee for a Human Life Amendment, Inc. Printed by permission of the author.

From: ABORTION IS NO MAN'S BUSINESS

Men have borne up well while forcing women to bear down in unwelcome labor and to bow down in lifetime subservience to the unwanted fruits of sex. Woman's condition of servitude has been rationalized in all sorts of ways; it has influenced our social and religious attitudes and has colored the male-dominated thinking of psychiatrists and psychoanalysts.

In all the consideration of abortion there has been almost no consideration of woman. She is regarded as nothing more than an encapsulating amniotic sac, and it is only the population explosion that has renewed interest in legalizing abortion. Demographer Christopher Tietze has noted the relationship between tolerance of abortion and the political wish to manipulate population size.

There was a time when survival of the species required that woman accept unwanted pregnancy. It is a measure of human absurdity that today, although our crowded planet will soon compel us to enforce limited reproduction for all, many still refuse to accept the limited population control that abortion offers . . . .

If we are going to legislate on issues of human reproduction—and of course we should not—then we ought to deal with the important issues for the individual and for society. We should not permit an unwanted child to be born. An unwanted child destroys a woman's mastery of her life and creates great stress and anxiety, damaging to her and to all around her. But the real victim is the child. For we hide from the unpleasant fact that an unwanted child is a hated child and will be treated cruelly—by overprotection, by inattention, by destructiveness or abandonment, by child-battering, by murder. And ultimately society suffers: hated children become hate-filled adults, even more destructive to their own children . . . .

The procreative act is very different for man and for woman. Man's life continues essentially unchanged after sexual intercourse. If the woman is impregnated, her life is completely altered. And the role of the father is largely neglected. He has been an equal partner in procreation, sometimes has had a major share of the pleasure, and need accept virtually none of the responsibility.

This is obvious in the case of rape, but what about the complex uses of sexual intercourse in married life? Preventive and educational efforts should apply as much to the man as to the woman, although she is the necessary focus of attention.

When an unwelcome and unwanted pregnancy occurs, we refuse to restore a woman to her former state. We even bolster our lack of concern for her by insisting that she will be physically or psychologically damaged if we grant her relief.

149

We further insist that the potential child live, no matter how miserable or unpleasant the life may be . . . .

Psychiatrists—among them Robert Laidlaw, Arthur Peck and John M. Cotton—have suggested that the physical and mental dangers of therapeutic abortion have been highly exaggerated. There is an imbalance in the equation of traditional psychiatric thinking. Serious reactions to abortion are much fewer than serious reactions to unwanted pregnancy. This was confirmed when Richard Rappaport and Peter Barglow studied 35 women who had undergone therapeutic abortion. Seventy-five per cent of the women reported improved emotional status, which was confirmed by psychiatric evaluation; 23 per cent believed that the abortion led to their emotional growth; and only two women wished they had not chosen to abort. The real danger lies in the condition of the woman who is driven to self-induced or illegal abortion. These quests for abortion often take on the quality of hopeless struggles against unknown and unfathomable odds—the kind of struggles we associate with the works of Franz Kafka . . . .

Natalie Shainess, M.D. Reprinted from *Psychology Today* Magazine, May 1970. Copyright © 1970. Ziff-Davis Publishing Company. All rights reserved.

From: ABORTION EXPLOITS WOMEN

After centuries of being treated as objects, women are being presented the final mechanical insult as a constitutional right.

The strange compulsion for abortion is in reality the ultimate exploitation of women by immature men: technocrats, generally, imbued with a myopic sense of social awareness and unable to interpret or control their own sexuality . . . .

It is not surprise that Playboy Foundation money is now competing with Rockefeller Foundation money to promote the concept of permissive abortion. The rich man's solution has become the puerile male's solution and the last vestige of responsibility and commitment has disappeared.

It is the woman who has been deliberately misled by the male-dominated medical profession into thinking that abortion is merely contraception slightly postponed. The serious physical and psychic consequences of this self-serving deception are muted despite a wealth of medical literature from the United States and foreign countries . . . .

We find the medical technicians claiming the organs and bodies of the aborted children for human experimentation; some of them still alive. What horrible echoes are these from the recent past!

What can we expect from a society that can rationalize away the most fundamental of human values—the value of life? What is to become of a medical profession that subsitiues self-serving cliches for its ethics? What is to become of women who would ask the courts to institutionalize death as a legitimate tool for solving personal problems? Such a society is doomed to an unending spiral of violence if women do not change it.

Women must deny violence a legitimate place in our society by rejecting the first violence—abortion. The women of this society must say to puerile men that the game is over. You can no longer exploit our bodies either in your center fold or in your hospitals.

Gloria Heffernan, M.D., Women Concerned for the Unborn Child. From *The Chicago Tribune.* Reprinted by permission.

From: THINKING STRAIGHT ABOUT ABORTION

The temptation to put down quickly the abortionist view when it confronts us has led to certain short circuits in our ability to communicate. And at a time when antiabortion amendments petitions are circulating widely among evangelical Christians we need to think out our reasons for this keenly felt stand. In the days ahead we will have to be communicating more and more about this vital subject. We must do so without those short circuits that cut off our listeners before we make our point; we want to speak worthily, as God would have us. For if we don't explain our own minds, and God's, a little better than we sometimes have done, we may even lose our opportunity to make a difference—though we may not ultimately believe that we can frustratę God's purposes . . . .

So if stepping back for a minute will help at all, perhaps we can reexamine some of our tactics and our words. If we don't like this thing called abortion, let's untangle our strategy, so that our reasoning makes some better sense on its own grounds. First of all we need to avoid what lies closest at hand on such an issue, the use of emotionally charged words accompanied by a shaking of the head Trundling out words like "evil" and "disastrous" and "dangerous" just confuses the issue. Such words may give vent to how we feel about the subject, but we need to explain *why*. If abortion is undesirable, it must be so for soundly stated biblical reasons, reasons that even our listeners will say sound clear enough, if we have avoided the temptation to dismiss the issue emotionally, as hastily as possible, or by proof-texting our way around the real biblical underpinnings for our argument. Nothing short of careful biblical exegesis will do, exegesis that considers at least two things: not only the "moment" when human life originates, but, even more significantly, God's purpose in making man at all.

Some clear and well expressed understanding of the high purposes of God in creating man and offering life will then temper our handling of the medical facts in the abortion issue, so that we can in the same way stand back from emotional and judgmental phrases and let the medical information do its own work. Let us seek out objective medical research on the life-status of the fetus at the moment of conception. Such purely medical data, carefully rendered, should stand by itself; we shouldn't have to prop it up with moral judgments. For instance, if the live fetus disintegrates during suction abortion, let that information stand as an awesome fact to do its own work. But on the other hand, if some of the facts suggest that abortion is not as medically dangerous to the woman as we "wish" it were, for the sake of finding a deterrent to the practice, let's not juggle those facts to make it sound mysterious and fearful. Statistics say that the risk of abortion to the mother in the first twelve weeks of pregnancy is three times less than the risk to her in a full-term birth. Abortions in the early weeks, therefore, cannot be labeled "dangerous," and any such statements must be balanced against the risk of full-term births. What risk there is in abortion occurs during the twelve-to-twenty-week period rather than in the early weeks, and even that risk is proportionately small. To pretend otherwise would be shady, and unworthy of our calling.

We don't need that kind of an approach. It is unworthy of all we stand for in the name of Christ. And there are better reasons and approaches—real, human, important ones. Abortion can better be opposed because it hurts everyone, the mother and father as well as the fetus. We need soundly researched statistical analysis of the psychological aftereffects of abortion, rather than threatening statements about "how awful it is." We need carefully documented follow-up statistics. Let us have an informed sociologist to do our homework for us, and let us study his findings. For instance, let him question the parents of the aborted fetus three years later. Do they ever think about that never-born child? These awesome aspects will keep us from the lesser tactics.

The most dangerous thing we can do is to leave the issue at the purely emotional level, consciously or inadvertently introducing language that may permanently cloud the issue. For instance, we may announce that "abortion rates are high in Communist countries" or that "Hitler's regime practiced abortion," hoping to make the hearer respond, "If Communists and Nazis are for abortion, I know I'm not!" Such logical traps are a clear case of perpetuating "short circuits," and God deserves better.

If we are convinced about the real difficulties of abortion and prefer to stand for the God-given mandate of life, we must be sure we make ourselves clear to everyone who is listening, Christian and non-Christian. Christians have tender consciences and believe in the Word of God. But abortion hurts everyone, not just those who believe that Word. Let us come up with arguments that speak to everyone, not just to that closed circle of believers whom we represent. We cannot force our convictions upon anyone else, but we can at least offer clarity. We must have a carefully articulated "apologia," one whose language speaks to everyone, one that clarifies why it is God's plan that human life is too significant to interrupt, to accept or reject as one likes.

What if we should, by our careful preparation and clear thinking, actually convince someone *away* from abortion? That is only the beginning for us. We must be prepared as Christians to help that person face the difficult circumstances of her decision. It is not enough to congratulate ourselves that we have found a better argument and gotten rid of the logical fallacies surrounding it. It is not enough to say "Aha, I convinced her," and then go home. Choosing to bear a child is a hard and immense decision. Even the legitimate and long-desired child is not carried and borne easily by its mother. Every expectant mother needs compassion and reassurance during that long waiting period. We need to provide vital companionship and unusual reassurance, in the most *humane* way we can, for the one who chooses to bypass abortion and endure an initially unwanted pregnancy. Let us further *praise* the unwed mother who shows the courage *not* to try to correct one mistake with another. Enough of harsh and judgmental treatment from the Christian brotherhood. Such courageous women, and the men who choose to stand by them, demand our love.

Perhaps we can also activate our adoption and counseling services to do more to encourage unwed mothers to bear these children. Can these agencies work any more closely with Christian doctors in preabortion counseling to assure these women that their child has a future? Can the Christian doctors with antiabortion convictions seek out these agencies and initiate some new kind of help for the expectant mothers and their unborn children? And if both agencies and doctors are already doing some of these things to counteract the overwhelming abortion trend, are we adequately aware of them?

And as for the rest of us, let us learn to love without "dissimulation." If we know an unwed pregnant woman, let us show her compassion and kindness. We are more often reluctant to talk with her; we are embarrassed for her and confused about what to say. If she chooses to bear the child, we need to encourage her, to come out in her active support, Anyone willing to work out the consequences for an act, rather than avoid them, should be supported by the Christian. And if an unwed woman chooses not only to bear but to keep her child, let us still give her our emotional support and, even more, our material assistance, even though we might disagree with the latter decision. She is accepting the consequences for her action in a remarkable way.

But what of those whom we convince too late? We need even more compassion for the woman who undergoes an abortion and then too late learns to grieve over the decision. Let us remind ourselves and that person of the forgiveness and plentiful grace that Christ offers and that Christians daily offer on Christ's behalf. Let us not close the door on those who go ahead with abortion. There is still room for them in the company of God. Let us be sure we make room for them among ourselves, too.

Nancy B. Barcus, *Christianity Today*, January 17, 1975, pp. 8-10. Copyright 1975 by Christianity Today; reprints by permission.

ABORTION AND THE TRUE BELIEVER

Most of us learn sooner or later how wise it is not to debate with True Believers. Debate with them ends as an exercise in futility. What follows is therefore not an argument for abortion, either therapeutic or personal; nor is it a retort to the arguments of the antiabortionists. It is simply a comment, as from the sidelines or the balcony, on the debate—which is essentially over the question whether a fetus is a person or not and, consequently, what rights if any ought to be assigned to uterine life.

I

Thoughtful people, not just dull old philosophers, are always bemused when they learn how a medieval notion called "substance" enters into the abortion debate, lurking behind and beneath the rhetoric of the "right to life" forces.

Spokesmen for the Roman Catholic hierarchy, backed by one Lutheran Synod and most Orthodox Jews, say that a fetus is a person and that therefore abortion is murder, the killing of an innocent person. They claim that a human embryo or fetus is a person because it is potentially a person. By this they mean that the "substance" of a person is already present in a fetus or unformed human. How sound or valid is this "preformist" idea? Well, it is like saying that the house is in the blueprint, the statue is in the marble, the book is in the writer's conception of it, the oak is in the acorn— and by the same token, and *a fortiori*, the person is in the fetus.

The substance doctrine is the one that holds up the sacramental theology of "transubstantiation"—the belief that even though the wafer in the mass has the "accidents" of bread (its taste, color, consistency, cereal content), down underneath these accidents lies the real substance, the body of Christ, which cannot be seen or touched or tasted or smelled but is nonetheless *there*—not just prospectively or virtually but actually.

In the same way, it is contended, the verifiable properties of a fetus are admittedly not personal; it has no cerebration or memory or ability to communicate or self-consciousness. But these things are, after all, only accidents. The person is actually there, unverifiably ("mysteriously") yet knowably by faith. It follows of course that abortion is killing an innocent person; i.e., that abortion is murder.

The medieval theology of transubstantiation offers a kind of "objective" argument against abortion, if you can accept its ontology or supernaturalistic theory of material reality. Its basis lies solely in a faith assertion: in an unverifiable *belief* in something we might call a preformed person. However, if you accept the faith assertion of "substance" (a very big If, to be sure), the deductive argument from it may be said to be a "logical" one in the syllogistic sense. (All fetuses are persons; this is a fetus; therefore this is a person: everything hangs on the first premise.)

For those who believe in the metaphysics of substance and accidents, who are convinced that the medieval sacramental theology was a true account of real things, it makes sense to refuse to terminate fetal development. But one more assumption is required for the antiabortion argument. Even if you are willing to revive the medieval notion of the "homunculus" (a minuscule person down *in* the fetus, maybe even in the sperm or ovum), you still have to assume (judge) that life is the highest good (*summum bonum*), thus taking priority over all other values—health, quality of life, recources for well-being, and so on. This is a vitalistic ethics, and it makes human life sacrosanct, taboo, untouchable.

On examination, all of this comes down to two highly challengeable jumps in reasoning. They are known, among those who do not indulge in them, as the "error of potentiality" (taking what could be as what already is) and the "fallacy of the single cause" (seeing the constant, ignoring the variable).

Thomas Aquinas rejected this line of argument. He distinguished between life *in potentia* and *in sit* (in being), and held that the difference between potential humanness and actual humanness is an essential difference, not merely a superficial or accidental one. For St. Thomas, what changed the fetus from merely biological life into a person was the "infusion of the soul" or "animation"—which he, like Aristotle, thought takes place about the time of quickening.

Some Catholics still hold to that opinion, but the Vatican's official teaching has discarded it.

Among antiabortionists there is, it should be noted, an alternative position. A few of them claim to have a revelation of some kind, written either in a book or in their hearts, that God's eternal will has sanctified the fetus. This group does *not* take its stand on the metaphysical ground. It is amusing to observe how Protestants who fiercely reject the substance theory at the altar accept it in the uterus; they repudiate transubstantiation sacramentally but swallow it whole fetally.

These two antiabortion arguments, the one metaphysical and the other revelational, are fused together in the debate, yet in fact they are quite independent of each other. Some nontheists (a few humanists also, as well as Mahayana Buddhists and the like) accept the metaphysical position but not the revelational, while a few theistic debaters (for example, evangelical Protestants, Orthodox Jews, and Jains in India) reverse things, holding to a revelation without recourse to any metaphysics.

II

Leaving metaphysical and supernatural grounds altogether, we find another group who oppose abortion on a different basis: on ethical rather than either metaphysical or revelational premises. They take their stand on what *ought* to be rather than on what is or at least is believed to be. Their starting point is a *value* commitment. Their contention is that because the potential of a fetus is personal value, we ought to preserve the fetus when we can for the sake of what is not yet actual but presumably will come to be.

Once you stake your antiabortion case on values rather than on alleged facts not in evidence, on what ought to be rather than on what is, you are landed in the whole ethical problem of values and preferences and choices, the problem of relative values and of proportionate good. This is a radically different order of argument against abortion.

It is one thing to say, "No matter what else has to be sacrificed (health, happiness, growth, resources), I will not murder a 'substantially' real person"; but it is a quite different thing to say, "No matter what has to be lost in terms of present values, I will not weigh them against the future value of this embryo." The essential feature of this latter argument is not that it rests on moral rather than metaphysical or religious grounds but that it *always* gives a first-order value to a fetus regardless of the situation or circumstances. When this posture is combined with substance metaphysics, we have a True Believer whose dogmatism rules out any kind of pragmatic or responsible judgment about down-to-earth cases.

The great majority of us—doctors, nurses, patients, people as people—look at the abortion issue in ethical rather than metaphysical or revealed terms. But even if we regard it ethically, we cannot deal with abortion dogmatically or absolutistically or by universalized generalizations. Whether present human values should be traded off for or subordinated to future fetal values would depend on a responsible assessment of proportionate good. Approached in this way, a good case can sometimes be made for abortion, whether it happens to be for medical reasons or personal reasons.

Surely no law should be tolerated which forces the "substance" theory on those who do not find it reasonable, either in the fetus or in the sacrament. At the political level—at any rate, in a democracy—it is obvious that like the substance doctrine, the revealed and vitalist doctrines are very much matters of private opinion.

Opposition to abortion is certainly a part of the freedom of religious belief and practice we want to protect: people should be free to embrace it. But that freedom has to be protected for all, not just for some. It is difficult if not impossible to see how church metaphysics or divine revelations or individual value perferences can be imposed by law on those who do not believe them to be either true or wise.

This is, in a word, the recommendation of wise and thoughtful people on both sides of the opinion line—those who disapprove abortion as well as those who approve it.

LET'S GET HONEST ABOUT ABORTION

Some of the points raised by Joseph Fletcher in his November 27 article "Abortion and the True Believer" need to be challenged forcefully. Among other notable observations, he heaps scorn upon those who affirm that a person exists in the fetus. I hope to show that this question of the nature of the fetus simply cannot be allowed to stand as the crux of the ethical issue involved in abortion.

Further, Fletcher's likening this antiabortionist thought to the idea that a house exists in its blueprint misses, I think, one important difference. The homebuilders (moral agents) must perform many free, deliberate, purposive actions before there is *even the slightest possibility* of that blueprint's becoming a house. But in regard to the fetus's becoming a child, the homebuilders (moral agents) already have performed all possible free, deliberate, purposive actions to bring that about. Thus the only free, deliberate, purposive action left to them is the abortion—the violent interdiction—of the process they freely put into motion. That distinction ought not escape an ethicist whose specialty and reputation center on the free, deliberate, purposive actions of moral agents.

I

At the outset of this response, it is imperative to be clear about what we are biting off even before we begin to chew. I have no intention of developing here a full-fledged position regarding abortion, to counter Fletcher's observations or for any other purpose. I will not consider such exceptional situations as rape or those in which pregnancy threatens the

160

mother's life. Nor am I attempting any final ethical judgments; and, perhaps surprisingly, I do not propose to bring any Christian teaching or theology to bear.

My aim is much more modest: to see whether, by looking at two interpretations frequently adduced by the proponents of abortion, we can get the facts of the matter straight. Such would seem to be a proper first step; ethical and Christian reasoning, then, can and should proceed on the basis of the facts. But readers are cautioned not to ask more from this response than it offers to give.

In addition, there is a basic premise that should be stated at once: so far as *moral responsibility* is concerned, the man involved (the father-to-be) is just as much party to an abortion as is the woman (the mother-to-be). Of course, the fact that the man has no bodily stake in the operation itself makes it easy for him to evade his responsibility; but that does not change the truth of where the responsibility lies. Unless the man actively opposes the abortion and backs up that stance with appropriate offers of help, his moral position is no different from that of the woman who seeks the abortion. I am not prepared to torture the syntax here in order to make all the pronouns bilateral, but at every point we are addressing a problem of *human* morality, not female morality alone.

II

Almost all proabortion arguments start from the premise that the fetus which is acted upon is not a person, not a human being. The action itself, then, can be understood as private and personal—the woman acting upon herself, as it were, rather than acting upon another individual, since there is only one person involved, not two.

Mistakenly, I believe, the antiabortion forces have allowed this definition of the issue, have let it become the ethical horizon; thus they have put themselves under the necessity of arguing that the fetus is indeed a person, a real live human being. And so the battle rages: "It isn't!" "It is too!" "It is not!" "Why of course it is!" But because there is

161

no agreed-upon definition of what constitutes a human being and because there is no possible way of getting an ethically authoritative definition, we are condemned to a shouting match that has no chance of progress, is utterly futile, and can never be anything but an endless hassle.

However, my contention is that there is no need to hang up on this point or to go down this blind alley. One can let the proabortion interpretation stand; it does not at all affect the facts of the matter or the real nature of the ethical situation.

Think of a man who wires a dynamite charge into a car and then, after the victim blows himself to bits, argues in court that he cannot be held guilty: his placing the dynamite in the car was an entirely private act, there was no one else around and in fact, he didn't even detonate the charge—the victim did that himself when he turned on the ignition. What the bomber says is true, of course, but it is also completely irrelevant. Clearly, it is possible to take action against a particular person without its being necessary for that person to be present at the time. Similarly, even if the recipient of direct action is a nonhuman fetus, it is quite possible to understand that the ultimate intent of the action concerns a specific and particular *person*.

A different version of the story brings it closer to the case at hand. Put it that the man wants to prevent the victim from getting to his destination and so blows up a railway trestle and lets the train the victim is riding plunge into the abyss. This action is one intended to prevent the arrival of *a person on the way*. The significance of that last phrase is only slightly different in our two examples: with the bomber's action, it designates a person who is on the way to a place; with abortion, it designates a fetus on the way to becoming a person. But in either case the ultimate goal is to prevent the *arrival* of a particular *person*.

III

"A particular person": by the time of abortion, it has already been well determined *who* the person to be born will be. Understanding that fact is important. Even if the fetus is not considered a human being, it cannot be thought of as some sort of undefined blob that might become one thing but might equally well become something else—this or that, an entirely chancy upshot. Not at all: the "blueprint" is there; the genetic code already has determined the identity of the person-to-be—that person's intelligence, special gifts, physical makeup, human possibilities. Abortion is an action directed at a very particular person.

And that person, it must be said, is very much "on the way." It is not necessary to maintain that an already-existent person is on the way to somewhere; it is sufficient to say that this person is on the way into existence. Just as it is possible that something could have prevented the train passenger's arrival even if the trestle had not been bombed, so is it possible that the fetus might not make it to personhood even if there were no abortion. Yet, as the arrival of the passenger was such a foregone conclusion that bombing seemed the only way to prevent it, so abortion is performed as the only means of preventing the arrival of this person who is on the way. In this regard, the customary phrase "an unwanted pregnancy" is quite misleading; the bomber, with as much justification, could speak of "the unwanted bridge" he was going to remove. No, in both cases the intended end of the action is the elimination of a specific unwanted *person*.

Consider that fetuses on the way to personhood do not require outside help to get where they are headed; they will make it on their own, as it were. Far from needing permission or help, the only way the fetus's arrival can be *stopped* is through violent interdiction.

In this regard, contraception is entirely distinct from abortion. Before conception, nothing has been determined as to "who" the person would be or even whether a person "should be." Indeed, there is no possibility of a person's getting under way *except* with the permission and help of the parents. At this point, the decision, control and responsibility are entirely theirs. But after conception, the only power they control is, as we have said, violent interdiction of the definite person who is definitely on the way.

IV

The second proabortion argument which needs to be examined is that a woman has the right to freedom of control over her own body. Here I would be most insistent on including the man—even to the extent of speaking in terms of "*their* control over *their* body." Her body has ceased to be solely her own; he has invested himself in it, whether either of them chooses to acknowledge that fact or not. The woman gave herself to the man as much as he gave himself to her, and neither has the right to act as though no mutuality were involved.

It seems apparent that this argument begins by assuming the previous one; namely, that fetuses bear no necessary relationship to human beings, that only one person—the woman—is involved, that all is to be comprehended under the term "her own body." I have disputed that assumption above; however, even if it were granted, this second argument is still faulty. The truth of the matter is that the woman *did* have freedom of control over her own body. But shift now into the more accurate wording: they had the freedom of control over *their* body, and they chose to exercise that freedom in a particular way. In the event of pregnancy, their demand is not for the right to "freedom" but for the right to renege on responsibility for the freedom already exercised. It is as if someone freely jumped off the diving board and then suddenly demanded his right not to get wet. Freedom and irresponsibility are not the same concept; quite the contrary, true freedom must imply and entail responsibility.

V

Now that the argument has called to our attention the issue of personal freedom, we can be grateful, for the focus should be moved away from abortion and directed to that part of the proceedings where freedom *is* a reality. Indeed, I wonder whether any church or organization has the right to render a judgment regarding abortion—either pro or con—until it has witnessed to, educated for, and helped in the direction of that responsible use of sexual freedom which would eliminate most of the need and desire for abortion. Yet this we have not done. We live in a society that advocates sexual irresponsibility under the guise of "freedom"; responding out of a fear of being prudish and old-fashioned, we choose conformity—or at least silence Inevitably, then, both the unsympathetic prohibitions of those who oppose abortion and the humanitarian sentimentalities of those who justify it take on a very hollow ring.

Yet the proper economy of sexual freedom is this: sexual intercourse is a gift, a human *privilege* desired for the pleasure and satisfaction it provides. But just as the license for the privilege of driving on our highways entails the acceptance of liability for any accidents that ensue, so the ethical license for sexual freedom entails responsibility for consequences. However, modern people do not like the idea of responsibility, and the church isn't doing much to challenge them with it.

Freedom to abort ("to control her own body") is only one small feature of the broad move toward sexual freedom (irresponsibility) that is sweeping our society. The church would do well to confront this philosophy at its source rather than merely argue over the one detail.

There are any number of ethical, humanitarian and Christian concerns that bear upon the abortion issue, both pro and con, and that call for attention. However, any discussion of them cannot get very far unless it is based on an honest, factual understanding of what abortion is and what it signifies. We need God's guidance as we proceed to seek his will.

Vernard Eller. Copyright 1975 Christian Century Foundation. Reprinted by permission from the January 1-8, 1975 issue of *The Christian Century*, pp. 16-18.

CHAPTER 13
From the Scripture

The word "abortion" does not appear in the Bible. In writings about the issues related to abortion the following Bible passages are often used.

Exodus 21:22-25: When men strive together, and hurt a woman with child, so that there is a miscarriage, and yet no harm follows, the one who hurt her shall be fined, according as the woman's husband shall lay upon him; and he shall pay as the judges determine. If any harm follows, then you shall give life for life, eye for eye, tooth for tooth, hand for hand, foot for foot, burn for burn, wound for wound, stripe for stripe.

Judges 13:3-5: And the angel of the Lord appeared to the woman and said to her, "Behold, you are barren and have no children; but you shall conceive and bear a son. Therefore beware, and drink no wine or strong drink, and eat nothing unclean, for lo, you shall conceive and bear a son. No razor shall come upon his head, for the boy shall be a Nazirite to God from birth; and he shall begin to deliver Israel from the hand of the Philistines."

Job 3:3: "Let the day perish wherein I was born, and the night which said, 'a man-child is conceived.' "

Job 3:7-10: "Yes, let that night [of his conception] be barren; let no joyful cry to heard in it. Let those curse it who curse the day, who are skilled to rouse up Leviathan. Let the stars of its dawn be dark; let it hope for light, but have none, nor see the eyelids of the morning; because it did not shut the doors of my mother's womb, nor hide trouble from my eyes."

Job 3:16: "Or why was I not as a hidden untimely birth, as infants that never see the light?"

Psalm 36:9: For with thee is the fountain of life; in thy light do we see light.

Psalm 51:5: Behold, I was brought forth in iniquity, and in sin did my mother conceive me.

Psalm 104:29, 30: When thou hidest thy face, they are dismayed; when thou takest away their breath, they die and return to their dust. When thou sendest forth thy Spirit [or breath] they are created; and thou renewest the face of the ground.

Psalm 127:3: Lo, sons are a heritage from the Lord, the fruit of the womb a reward.

Psalm 139:13-16: For thou didst form my inward parts, thou didst knit me together in my mother's womb. I praise thee, for thou art fearful and wonderful. Wonderful are thy works! Thou knowest me right well; my frame was not hidden from thee, when I was being made in secret, intricately wrought in the depths of the earth. Thy eyes beheld my unformed substance; in thy book were written, every one of them, the days that were formed for me, when as yet there was none of them.

Ecclesiastes 11:5: As you do not know how the spirit comes to the bones in the womb of a woman with child; so you do not know the work of God who makes everything.

Isaiah 44:2: Thus says the Lord who made you, who formed you from the womb and will help you: Fear not, O Jacob my servant, Jeshurun whom I have chosen.

Isaiah 49:1: Listen to me, O coastlands, and hearken, you peoples from afar. The Lord called me from the womb, from the body of my mother he named my name.

Jeremiah 1:4, 5: Now the word of the Lord came to me saying, "Before I formed you in the womb I knew you, and before you were born I consecrated you; I appointed you a prophet to the nations."

Luke 1:41-44: And when Elizabeth heard the greeting of Mary, the babe leaped in her womb; and Elizabeth was filled with

167

the Holy Spirit and she exclaimed with a loud cry, "Blessed are you among women, and blessed is the fruit of your womb! And why is this granted me, that the mother of my Lord should come to me? For behold, when the voice of your greeting came to my ears, the babe in my womb leaped for joy."

Acts 17:24, 25: The God who made the world and everything in it, being Lord of heaven and earth, does not live in shrines made by man, nor is he served by human hands, as though he needed anything, since he himself gives to all men life and breath and everything.

Galatians 1:15: But when he who had set me apart before I was born, and had called me through his grace . . .

Galatians 5:13: For you were called to freedom, brethren; only do not use your freedom as an opportunity for the flesh, but through love be servants of one another.

Philippians 1:21-24: For to me to live is Christ, and to die is gain. If it is to be life in the flesh, that means fruitful labor for me. Yet which I shall choose I cannot tell. I am hard pressed between the two. My desire is to depart and be with Christ, for that is far better. But to remain in the flesh is more necessary on your account.

CHAPTER 14
For Further Reading

Numerous books are available regarding abortion and related issues. Rather than an extended bibliography, which would be out of date several months after publication anyway, this chapter includes reviews of selected books. (Also note that the sources of all materials quoted in chapters 11 and 12 are given; so readers may write for the complete article or book.) The books included in this chapter were chosen because they present specific views that offer another dimension to abortion counseling.

ABORTION: The Personal Dilemma by R. F. R. Gardner, ed., Eerdmans Publishing Co., Grand Rapids, Mich., 1972, $5.95.

Gardner is both a consultant gynecologist and an ordained minister. He writes as a committed Christian. His work is a complete and realistic examination of the abortion issue.

"All decisions on abortion are religious decision," states the author. He feels that the church has failed to give proper Christian guidance on the subject. "Too many [pregnant women] have died because moralistic clergymen and the mercenary underworld have driven them into the hands of unskilled individuals."

He recognizes that when the church speaks out on a subject it is often criticized as a busybody. Yet the witness of the church is necessary and silence is mistaken for approval. He also feels that theologians are often inconsistent in their view of life. He illustrates this with those who properly praise Dietrich Bonhoeffer as the heroic pacifist who saw it his duty to plot against Hitler's life yet do not listen to Bonhoeffer's condemnations of abortion.

Perhaps chapter 15, "The Lesser Evil?" is the most challenging and significant section of Gardner's book. As a Christian physician he feels there are times he must assist in abortion; though his general stance is against termination of pregnancy. Yet he will not perform an abortion as a lesser of two evils. He writes:

"It seems to be, therefore, that the Christian must so consider each case that he can see his abortions, as he sees his cesarean sections, as among, 'those good deeds which God hath before ordained that we should walk in them.' Deeds done, in Christ's name, for Christ's sake. These are daunting words to write, but having once agreed that some abortions are right I can see no other attitude which does not deny the central meaning of the Christian life."

Abortion and Social Justice edited by Thomas W. Hilgers and Dennis J. Horan, eds., Sheed & Ward, New York, 1973, $1.95.

A 16-chapter collection of opinions on the medical, legal, and social aspects of abortion—along with full-color pictures of a fetus before and after abortion. Male counselors might find it helpful to read chapter 11, "Now Why Not Ask a Woman?"

All counselors should read chapter 13, "Abortion, Poverty, and Black Genocide: Gifts to the Poor?" for a point of view often ignored in a middle-class, white discussion about abortion.

In "Private Individual vs. Global Village" Marshall McLuhan writes: "If the rights of the individual are to be measured quantitatively against the needs and pressures of society, there can be no serious disagreement. The individual must go. If the good, private or corporate, is to be measured quantitatively, the lesser must always yield to the greater. (In Christianity at least, there is no question of quantity. Human rights are grounded in a divine source which overcomes all mere quantitative differences.)"

Handbook on Abortion by Dr. and Mrs. J. C. Willke, Hiltz Publishing Co., Cincinnati, Ohio, 1973, $1.25.

A hard hitting, emotional and unapologetic attack against abortion under any circumstances. Shows full-color pictures of an abortion under the heading "Killed by Abortion."

Dr. and Mrs. Willke write in a straightforward, question-and-answer style. They deal with every issue—including incest and rape—in a chapter that ends, "And finally, isn't it a twisted logic that would kill an innocent, unborn baby for the crime of his father?"

This book represents an extreme position that must be considered. However, the book should not be given to a person who has had or who is considering an abortion. Rather let its message be shared through the experiences of a loving counselor.

MANDATORY MOTHERHOOD: The True Meaning of "Right to Life" by Garrett Hardin, Beacon Press, 1974, $1.95.

Written to oppose the proposed "Right To Life" constitutional amendment, this book stresses the advantages of a society where abortions are safe, legal, and secured without delay. Written with the emotional drive found in *Handbook on Abortion,* but from the other side of the issue.

Hardin sees life as a continuum with only one beginning; therefore he discounts any discussion to the question "Why does life begin?" in the development of a fetus. He also predicts problems that would arise (regarding taxes, inheritance, burial, etc.) if an unborn fetus were given status as a legal person.

Abortion and the Meaning of Personhood by Clifford E. Bajema, Baker Book House, Grand Rapids, Mich., 1974, $3.95.

Though his chapter title "When Is Man a Person?" seems out of date, the content raises and deals with important issues.

The author's premise is that all people are basically prolife. Either abortion is accepted by many because of difficult circumstances which make it seem like the lesser of two evils or abortion is endorsed as a side issue for those who have strong political and philosophical positions on other related issues.

Abortion Counseling and Social Change by Arlene Carmen and Howard Moody, Judson Press, Valley Forge, Pa., 1973, $2.95.

As two subtitles indicate ("From Illegal Act to Medical Practice" and "The Story of the Clergy Consultation Service on Abortion"), this book tells the story of clergy who were concerned about abortion counseling back in the days when it was illegal to help anyone terminate a pregnancy.

The book is a low-key presentation of human concerns for those who want abortions and traces the history of the movement from a few people at Judson Memorial Church in New York to the development of a national organization.

ABORTION: The Agonizing Decision by David R. Mace, Abingdon, 1973, $3.75, paper $1.95.

Mace's book on decision-making regarding abortion is basic for the counselor's library. It includes background material on abortion, case studies, and the questions that must be faced by one considering the possibility of terminating a pregnancy.

Situation Ethics, The New Morality by Joseph Fletcher, The Westminster Press, Philadelphia, Pa., 1966, paper $1.95.

Any person who opposes abortion on some grounds but grants the possibility of abortion on others will be accused of "situation ethics." Fletcher does use abortion as an example of a moral issue that must be determined by the situation. Unfortunately, the concept of situation ethics can often be misused. This book can be a help to the person who struggles under the freedom of the Gospel.

[1] Helmut Thielicke, *The Ethics of Sex*, trans. John Doberstein (New York: Harper & Row, 1964), pp. 237-238.

[2] Dietrich Bonhoeffer, *Ethics*, ed. Eberhard Bethge (New York: Macmillan, 1955), p. 130 (paperback ed. p. 175).

[3] Thielicke, p. 231.

[4] Ibid., p. 226

[5] Ibid., p. 224

[6] Bonhoeffer, p. 137 (paperback 183).

[7] Thielicke, p. 227.

[8] Bonhoeffer, p. 130 (paperback 175).